SOWN IN EARTH

Camino del Sol
A Latina and Latino Literary Series

SOWN IN EARTH

Essays of Memory and Belonging

FRED ARROYO

THE UNIVERSITY OF
ARIZONA PRESS
TUCSON

The University of Arizona Press
www.uapress.arizona.edu

ISBN-13: 978-0-8165-3951-2 (paper)

Cover design by Leigh McDonald
Cover photo: Fred with Hat and Beach © Fred Arroyo
Designed and typeset in Baskerville Com 10/15 by Leigh McDonald

Publication of this book is made possible in part by the proceeds of a permanent endowment created with the assistance of a Challenge Grant from the National Endowment for
the Humanities, a federal agency.

Library of Congress Cataloging-in-Publication Data
Names: Arroyo, Fred, 1966– author.
Title: Sown in earth : essays on memory and belonging / Fred Arroyo.
Other titles: Camino del sol.
Description: Tucson : The University of Arizona Press, 2020. | Series: Camino del Sol, A
    Latina and Latino Literary Series
Identifiers: LCCN 2019017184 | ISBN 9780816539512 (paperback)
Subjects: LCSH: Puerto Ricans—United States. | Hispanic American men. | LCGFT:
    Essays.
Classification: LCC PS3601.R725 S69 2020 | DDC 814/.6 —dc23
LC record available at https://lccn.loc.gov/2019017184

Printed in the United States of America
♾ This paper meets the requirements of ANSI/NISO Z39.48-1992 (Permanence of Paper).

LIVING WITH SHADOWS

Birds are singing as they have
every day since spring.
The river lazes downstream brown from rain.
They all say whoever lives here
lives in Paradise.
I've made the best of it
but the summer is short-lived.
Already the sunflowers turn face down,
I think of fall and the chill river winds.
A large moth settles on my forehead.
I will not make it move.

—PABLO MEDINA, ARCHING INTO THE AFTERLIFE

Contents

PART I. CONNECTICUT

85 Reed Avenue	9
Dracula	21
Intervals: If I Were a Bell	23
Roytype	31
World on a String	34
Peppers	37
Patina	40
Newfoundland	42
How My Father Taught Me to Write	48
Like a Thief in the Night	52

PART II. MICHIGAN

Trash Truck	59
Puerto Rican House	65
Almost Blue	73
Always True	81

Blue in Green   86

Farmer's Creek   97

Sown in Earth   118

Blue Memory   135

PART III. ISLAND

Up Jumped Spring   141

Ox in the Dusk   145

Ají Dulce   154

Patio Dreams   160

PART IV. OUT OF THIS WORLD

Grand Marais   171

Next Country   195

Album   208

Working Days   218

Nights in the Gardens of Spain   223

Calle de Santiago   235

Sofrito   247

Freight   251

Pulsar Watches   254

Blood Work   256

Other Side of Memory   265

Paraíso   267

Acknowledgments   *269*

SOWN IN EARTH

My father lying in a snowbank. Without a frown or smile, the side of his face calm, his legs and arms positioned as if he had been running or lifting a heavy box or sack. His dark brown silk shirt patterned in oranges and yellows, a tapestry of suns, pineapples, mangoes, the sleeves perfectly folded back to his elbows, his hands cupped at his lips from holding a bottle or calling out a name. Looking at his bare arms I knew that no matter how drunk he was, my father must be cold, his face beginning to blue.

What happened to his coat?

He can stay out there and freeze. My mother stared out the window. It'll do him some good.

Someone had dropped him off. He got out of the car and headed up the walkway to the front porch. A Saturday afternoon. He turned back, as if to wave, and fell just before the front porch, the snow, perhaps, softening his fall.

A state trooper stood over my father, tried to rouse him, get him to stand. He bent and pulled my father's arm over his shoulder, wrapped his arm around his waist, and brought him to his feet, my father's knees still bent and wet with snow. With the trooper at his side, my father slowly made it up the stairs and into the living room. He staggered, pushed back his shoulders, slurred *I'm okay okay okay*. His head dropped and he started to moan and weep. The leather of the trooper's gun belt and boots creaked, his uniform tight, pressed, clean. He was a giant next to my father's bent and loose body. In a hard encouraging voice he said, *You'll be okay, that's right, okay*, as he gently led my father to the couch and guided him to lie down.

I had seen my father drunk before. I had waited late into the night for my father to come home. Sitting on a chair with my legs thrown over the arm, half asleep, almost dreaming, when he stumbled through the door smelling of rum and cigarettes. That Saturday was the first time I laughed, and when the sounds escaped from my mouth I started to become someone else. I witnessed him with the eyes of distance and closeness, the eyes of a camera saving what would last forever, and I felt the silence between us grow inside me, felt its weight pushing against my chest, and wondered if this is how the roaring of words begins. I stood at the window, let the images and silence overtake me: my father passed out in the snow.

Chago, you will always be my father . . . The words disappeared and he became any man freezing in the snow, a man I could look upon with grief and forgiveness, no matter if the world expected much more.

I don't remember saying good-bye. I don't remember his leaving. He was there asleep on the couch, my mother saying good-bye to the state trooper, closing the door, and the next day my father was gone.

There is an old photograph in a thick, lime green album just wide enough to hold three-by-five photos, and when I open it each photo is in a plastic sleeve, the photos lying one on top of the other, and like they're a deck of cards on a felt table, I run my finger up and down the plastic sleeves, barely revealing a photo, and when I stop this shuffling, one image appears colorful and clear. My father, standing in the kitchen door wearing a long black wool coat, a black hat with a shiny black band and a wide brim tilted back a bit off his forehead, and his hand caught in midair after releasing the tan suitcase on the floor. His hands the dark brown of a cup of coffee with a thin line of condensed milk stirred within. His face just as brown, his high cheekbones burnished red, and his smile filled with nothing other than joy. He had gone back to Puerto Rico, and now he had returned. My father, Chago, came back home.

I should've gotten out of bed, gone to my table, and written the dream down. I lay there listening to the birds just before first light and let the dream play over and over. Snow fell through the wet catalpa tree. Green and blue glinted off the trooper's pistol reflecting the ornaments on the Christmas tree in the corner of the living room. My father's arm fell off the couch, his hand open, his crooked fingers almost touching the carpet, the deep lines crisscrossing his palm, his arm reddened from the snow. This dreaming continued on, the images and details growing, and as I fought the need to sleep, I found I was standing at a window looking out past a tree, over an avenue, and into a field—looking, waiting, beginning to remember. Snow. Images. Winter. Details. Remembering. It is always true.

Part I
CONNECTICUT

85 Reed Avenue

My father found a house to rent on 85 Reed Avenue, and next door, on the corner of the avenue, there was a monument sales office. A large yard of lush green grass, a split-rail fence, and studded in a maze across the lawn were gray, red, and white gravestones. Running through the yard was a narrow, smooth black road. I made this mock graveyard my own. A lilac bush stood at one end near the house, and a few scattered, thin trees that flowered in the spring. A stone bench sat in the middle, and I could sit there forever and listen to the wind gathering in a hush in the tops of the trees, watch the sun striking the face of a gravestone, a square shadow growing long on the other side. There was nothing morbid or frightening about playing here. There was no one to like or dislike, to yell, to throw a glass against a wall, to rap knuckles hard against the top of a head, or to speed away from. I watched the grass grow thick, listened to branches twisting in the wind, smoothed my hands along the rough, diamond-like edges of the bench with the gravestones bluing in the twilight.

At first it was simply a place to ride my bike through—quiet, smooth, back and forth on the black asphalt drive. That year at school we were studying the French and Indian War, and I fought on the side of the French as I crawled across the lawn, tomahawk in hand, hiding behind a stone, peering around the edge for the enemy, then crawling to the safe shadow of the next stone. Lying on my back, a blade of grass held up to the sky, time fell away as the blade conducted a parade of passing clouds. Gradually the mock graveyard changed. Something pushed me more and more from our house to search out its solitude and silence. Too many of my father's friends, too much family visiting, and with them the loud talking, the laughing, the clinking of bottles and glasses. In the first grade my parents had sent me away for a year to live in Michigan, and now I had to learn all over how to follow and speak Spanish with my father's family and friends. I felt they saw me as different, someone who had gone away, returned, and could never be the same, could never fully be a part of their lives. My father was distant, silent, easily angered. Many times I found him passed out on the brown couch in the living room. One morning he's vomiting in the bathroom, later he's pulling over the car, cracking open the door, retching in the street. Another morning he gingerly rises from the couch, can't move his neck, loudly moans and slams his glass on the counter—it hurts to swallow, to move his neck. Another morning a quart-size Ball jar filled with hot water, wrapped in a dishtowel, and placed behind his lower back as he lies on the couch.

It's not your back that's sore—you're ruining your liver, my mother said.

Away from the house and the couch, outside, I could forget, the graveyard becoming a clean, sure, and sober escape. The war only in my imagination.

*
**

I had returned from Michigan to my next country, a place where my childhood comes to life here on the edge of an industrial park on 85 Reed Avenue in West Hartford, Connecticut. My parents rented the small white house with an acre of land from an Italian contractor, and the contractor had built at the end of the driveway a storage space for his construction equipment made of high stockade fencing with a locked gate. It looked like a fort and was big enough to park a few trucks inside. I made a small baseball diamond in the backyard, and for some reason I placed first base on the left side and ran the bases in reverse. I tossed the ball up, gripped the bat with both hands, swung as the ball dropped by, and began running around the bases once I had knocked the ball out into the yard, my dropped bat rattling against the packed dirt of home plate. First base was a long plank butted against a stake and the top of the stockade fence, the plank supporting the fence because inside yellow scaffolding was stacked against it. I quickly stepped up the plank like a tightrope walker, leaped over the fence, and crawled across the scaffolding to drop down on the graveled ground. I walked the path around the edges lined with cement mixers, shovels and spades and pickaxes, concrete blocks and red bricks. There were things covered with blue tarps, stacks of lumber and plywood, the smell of pine and tar and oil, the dented bottom of an overturned wheelbarrow collecting rain and sparkling with rust.

My father was the oldest son. Each of his three brothers came in turn to the mainland and received his help. His brother Eddie worked at the Roytype Typewriter factory with my father for a time and lived with us before he was married. After the brothers became settled they were always stopping by with their families, as did my father's sister. In the summer, my grandmother came from Puerto Rico. That house on Reed Avenue was where my father's relatives would meet weekend after weekend, and we would load up our cars and drive to Ocean Beach Park in New London or head to

Marlborough and turn down a dirt road that led to a golden brown brook where we'd swim. Out in our backyard on the picnic table there would be pots of beans and rice, a plate stacked with thin, glistening pork chops, a bowl of potato salad, and bottles of beer and whiskey chilling in a cooler as everyone gathered for dinner. In the winter, drinks and plates of food spread from the kitchen to the living room, *plena* following voices and gestures. This was the house where my father's friends came to visit and drink, a kind of country house, a *finca*, an escape from the city.

In Hartford my father had attended school to become a mechanic. When a friend brought out his car, they would work on it in the driveway. There was one man who came every week or two with a new used car. He would buy a car, drive it for a bit, and then sell or trade it for another. These cars always needed a few repairs, and there was often a car up on blocks, the hood open, my father and his friend bent deep inside with a light overhead, or lying underneath, their ankles and feet twisting in the gravel as they pulled hard on a wrench or lifted a heavy part. In the afternoon men arrived with buckets of clams, some fish heads wrapped in butcher paper, plastic bags heavy with pink and blue octopi, or a skinned headless rabbit laid out in a pan. The kitchen filled with the sweet aromas of cilantro and paprika, the flurry of arms cutting onions and smashing garlic, the sound of a light simmer in the trembling lid of an aluminum pot. They'd sit on the front porch or out in the backyard at the picnic table, and they'd talk over steaming bowls and full glasses. And when my father had one of his great parties, even if it was meant for my birthday, his friends arrived with whiskey and rum, conversation and laughter, and on the edge of their animated voices I began to hear the importance of memory and story, and no matter how far you were from home, you could gather in the company of other men and bridge the endless, lonely distances you carried inside. Standing in our kitchen talking, raising their glasses, their eyes intense and watery with emotion, the windows on the back porch steaming from the heat of their bodies, these men had lives richer than their ink-stained hands and arms, their streaked foreheads and cheeks. When they left Roytype on a Friday evening and walked by like a parade, I sat in the backseat and read their names within the white patch on their navy blue uniform shirts, the script a thin cursive floating just above their hearts. These men who would never touch the keys of a typewriter, who would never see on a white sheet of paper the sudden stonelike tap of a colored letter from the ribbons they made and packed day after day.

We had no books in our house on Reed Avenue. I liked going to school, though, and discovered great pleasure in reading books from the library. Although I don't remember any details from these books, I can still see my young boy self on long, silent afternoons following George Armstrong Custer's days at West Point, Teddy Roosevelt in Cuba and Panama, General John J. Pershing leading his troops along the Southwest border, Huck Finn floating down the mighty Mississippi, and the smoke from guns and cannons hovering like a ribbon across the rolling battlefields in *The Red Badge of Courage*. A small, white library on New Britain Avenue. On Saturdays my mother would drop me off, and I'd sit at a wide table and read encyclopedia entries (page after thin page in the volume dedicated to *A*). Sometimes the library would show short films, and I felt the power of journeys, sickness, and love when I watched the enchanting *Velveteen Rabbit* and *Paddle to the Sea*. To this day my favorite time of year is late summer into the fall, when I can return to those days of beginning school, the bright sun, the changing leaves, the arrival of colder winds scattering colors on the ground. I'm sitting in the graveyard, leaning back against a stone, a book on my lap, my hand turning a page.

*⋆⋆

What was it that drove my father to drink with *gran fiebre*—a great fever? What caused him to stay out late into the night? What made him devastatingly sad, silent, and angry? Distant. Changing into someone I didn't know, someone who scared me. When I return to 85 Reed Avenue I can't remember what I could've done to drive my father from home. I didn't, at the age of five, take off for Michigan. My parents made the decision to send me away.

They married young, my mother seventeen, my father twenty-one, and when I was born the next year they began a series of moves: Three Rivers, Michigan, back to Niles, Michigan, Niles to Chicago, Illinois, Chicago back to Niles, and Niles to Hartford, Connecticut. Even though neither had graduated from high school, they both enrolled in a social program that helped my father attend a technical school to learn automotive repair and my mother a training initiative that offered her a job with the Bell Telephone Company. There were years with very little money, lean, hungry years. There were times when they were turned away by landlords because my father was Puerto Rican. Perhaps there was something more exciting and free my father imagined outside marriage and family. Perhaps after already working since the third grade he started to wonder how many jobs he might still need to apply for, how many apartments he might be denied. Perhaps it was only in the night—at a bar, standing in a pool hall, sitting in a dark kitchen with a bottle of rum—that he recognized himself. Out, away, meeting up with his friends, talking to new people, remembering work and cars and travel, out away from home he might have heard his voice. And he could forget that no one ever offered him a job as a mechanic.

I have no legend to interpret my childhood map. All I have is the map's fleeting *topoi*: across from our house on 85 Reed Avenue was a factory that made some mysterious substance. In the evenings and on Sundays, when the factory was not in production, I'd ride my bike down the blacktop drive and around the factory to the other side, where there was a compound encircled with a tall barbed wire fence. Inside were hundreds of sealed barrels. Close to the fence was one with its lid loose, and I poked my finger through the fence and touched a spongy goo, my fingerprint instantly set in the soft black tar. I had recently watched an episode of *60 Minutes* that had something to do with the FBI and fingerprints. For days I trembled with fear, my stomach roiling with chaotic butterflies. I rode around the building again and again, and on each pass of the barrel my fingerprint was still there, as was the vague sensation of tar stuck to my fingertip. Sunday evening, the quiet lull between the end of the weekend and the return to school. My mother sitting on a chair and darning a pair of socks and a shirt. My father's out. I'm rubbing my finger against my palm, digging deep within for courage. Finally I raise the question of how fingerprints work, and as we talk I reveal what I had done, as if putting my finger in that open barrel will haunt me for the rest of my life, because somehow that spongy tar will remember me forever.

You're worried over nothing—you didn't do anything wrong. My mother laughs, shakes her head. *You better stay away from those barrels, and don't touch anything having to do with that factory.*

On the other side of the factory, a wide, long field, one side bounded by weeds and trees, the other side by a road, and at the end a clump of willows, a brook, and the tenements of Hartford in the distance. It was a strange field—tall grasses and weeds grew, along with large patches of purple clover I pulled from the ground to feed my rabbits—but it was mostly blacktopped, and the plants had to push their way out through the black-and-gray cracks. A testing ground, I imagined, a kind of laboratory where the factory spread out its formulas and experiments, creating trial roads and parking lots from the mysterious tarlike substance contained in those barrels.

In our front yard, standing near the catalpa tree, I looked across the field to where it turned into a dry plain. In the distance the outline of Cedar Mountain, and I dreamed again of one day hiking to the top, turning back, and catching a glimpse of our house, the gravestones small as pebbles, and then turning again to look out toward the Atlantic. I crossed Reed Avenue and walked through the weeds, grasses, and clover, the different versions of asphalt looking like black crooked streams and rivers, a wide gray-and-black sea. I crossed a road and stood on a dusty bank above the meandering brook.

There, up on a stone foundation, was a small red house with short windows looking down on the brook and across the plain. I wondered if it were some kind of lock or lookout, perhaps a pumping station. Walking by I waited for someone to exit the house, yell *halt*. I stared hard at the ground, felt my feet hit the hard dirt and gravel. No one came out, and at the end of the road I turned right, crossed over the brook onto another desolate road that led to the sound of growing traffic, smelled warm oil and sugar, and reached the parking lot of the Mr. Donut on the corner of New Britain Avenue. Across the avenue was my destination: a pink-and-green-neon-lit drugstore, where I thumbed through the comics, read several, and if I had saved up enough change, chose the one I wanted to take home.

Around the corner from our house was the Columbia Music Hall. Friday night in the graveyard, the outline of Cedar Mountain blurry in blue and pink, the music giant with bass and cheers, my feet cool in the grass, the sky full of bright stars. The music and cheers rolled on like thunder. On Saturday I rode my bike to the parking lot, picked up a stack of the tossed-away tickets from the confetti of white on the ground and slowly read their black script. I read each ticket and tried to memorize the typeface. There in the permanence of ink, no matter that the wind would blow the tickets away, that rain and snow would help them to disappear, there was a legend I tried to listen to.

*
**

My father cried out on the couch, his hands shaking after he punched the air, and then all quiet and still. He rolled over, his face against the back of the couch, and I heard a few coins fall from his pocket and clink against each other. A few twisted and crumpled dollars lay on the edge of the couch. I stepped closer, picked them up, and smoothed them out against my thigh. I grabbed the change and slipped the money in my back pocket. Underneath the edge of the couch was my father's wrinkled paper bag full of money, the edges of its mouth crinkled and soft, bright with silver within. I reached down and touched the cold metal, jerked away as if it burned. I reached down again and pulled it from underneath the couch. There were stacks of ones and fives in the bag, and a long-barreled gun I now held in my hand. The heavy handle had wooden grips, and the rest was silver and shiny. I pointed it at the couch, just above my father's shoulder, and looked down the barrel to the sight, one eye open, one eye closed.

I don't know what my father did for the syndicate. All I have are my memories of the carbon receipt books he brought home from Roytype and how I loved his clean and clear printing in the lines of numbers he wrote in three columns up and down the receipt pages. One night, many years later, just before sleep, the image of those receipt books filled with numbers burned elegantly in my mind. The story I heard the most about my father was that he had to quit school in the third grade to begin working, and yet here were these books filled with his tidy handwriting—and all the people he had met, talked to, and laughed with as he sold them numbers. My father, a *bolitero*.

A large man in a gray suit lies in a casket, his hands folded over his stomach, his face covered in a fine dusting of powder and rouge. My father's brother's wife, the daughter of the dead man, sobs uncontrollably. The parlor is full of mourners—sitting in folding chairs close to the casket, standing against the wall in groups, whispering. My uncle's father-in-law: death encountered for the first time. He looks at peace, but he had been standing in a phone booth talking to his mistress, was someone high up in the syndicate, when someone drove by with a machine gun and riddled his body with bullets. If he had survived the shooting, he'd be in a wheelchair for the rest of his life. Was that my father or mother speaking? It didn't matter. In the end he was dead.

Once my father had passed out, and in the morning his money bag wasn't there. Lost. Forgotten somewhere. Taken. Nowhere to be found in his car. He was nervous, his hands and shoulders shaking, pacing around the house, crazy trying to remember, trying to figure out what to do.

The raised sight becomes very clear, the edges of the metal rough and scratched, everything in the background blurry. I stand over my sleeping father trying to figure out what to do with the gun. My hands shake. I grip the gun handle harder, let it fall to my side, the pistol heavy, hot, and solid. Just before my hand fell, as the weight began to grow, my lips moved: *Bang-bang. Bang-bang. Bang.* My father doesn't move. I place the gun on top of the bag of money, put them on the floor in front of the couch where my mother can easily see them. She'll know what to do.

***

85 Reed Avenue. The shape of the narrow driveway through the mock graveyard. The dark green lawn and the thin flowering trees in the late spring wind. The stone bench. Listening to the birds, the

twisting trees. Following the clouds as they moved and changed—
rabbit, car, island, cloud, gun. This small place, a map I can return to
in memory and find everything in order, unchanged, not a blade of
grass out of place, and each gravestone still without a date or a name.

I hated to make my father angry, was careful of everything I did.
My stomach would ache, awash in nervous tension, as I worried
over being good. When we had lived in Hartford, I'd hung out with
a young man on the street and would mimic the things he did. He'd
leap up on the fender of a car, sit and watch the neighborhood pass
by, listen to the talk. I tried to do the same. I grabbed the car's
antenna to swing myself up and bent it in half. My father had to go
out and buy an antenna and replace it, his face burning with rage.
There was a bare wood column in the middle of our kitchen. My
father's thin leather strap hung from a nail. He took it down and
beat me, especially along my back and shoulders, to keep me in
line, to settle me down, and to remember his lost money, the extra
work he had to do, to sear that broken antenna with every stinging
whip into my memory.

I knew everything was better alone. I loved sitting against a
gravestone, my legs spread out in front of me on the grass, following the curves of cut stone with my open hands, crawling under
the split-rail fence, and riding my bike back and forth along the
graveyard road. Evenings, late Saturday, and Sunday afternoons
the graveyard became my sanctuary. In the twilight I watched the
grass turn from bright purple to the darkest of greens, felt the stone
smooth and cool against my shoulders. I followed the light as shadows thickened the spaces between the gravestones. Silence pulsed
within me, emptied my mind, the images of my father's drinking
and the noise of family and friends disappearing. I discovered the
peace of robins hopping in the grass, the sounds of distant traffic
becoming not just a backdrop but a part of the night beginning to
rise in the sky, bright stars beginning to appear.

I close my eyes, see the warehouses, factories, and loading docks that surrounded our house on 85 Reed Avenue. In the distance, yellow lights spark on in the tenement windows, the sky smudging from pink to orange to blue. I'm still, quiet, hard as the gravestones, and then I become smooth and inklike as I spread into the shadows thickening all around me.

The house on 85 Reed Avenue is empty. My father and his brothers had backed the moving truck close to an incline in the neighbor's backyard, placed two planks between the back of the truck and the incline, and then drove my mother's yellow Volkswagen Bug across the planks and up into the front of the truck. They filled the rest of the truck with the contents of the house. The next morning, around 4:30, my parents plan to get on the road for Michigan: they've decided to move back to where my mother's family lives, to where she and my father first met, to where I was born. I spread a blanket on the floor in a closet, add a pillow and another blanket. Curled up inside, with the door closed, I sleep.

My mother had asked me if I was sure I wanted to sleep there. It would get hot, she said, and I didn't have to. I said I wanted to. I felt I was ready to move, ready to leave 85 Reed Avenue. Go back to Michigan, where I had been exiled. This time maybe I could get everything right. Maybe I could help my mother and father find a home.

Dracula

There on the front porch of 85 Reed Avenue, sitting on the top step, was a man dressed in black—his boots, his slacks, his shirt all a clean, rich black. He had long '70s hair down to his collar, a thick Spanish mustache, and on the right side of his temple, as if a stone was growing from his skull, a large knot. He sat in contemplation, sad, perhaps suffering from a hangover, simply alone. A glistening bottle of Miller beer sat on the lower step between his legs. He looked out across the yard and avenue—in the distance, at the end the field, a cluster of weeping willows—his dark eyes still. I looked too and waited for the willows' tendrils to stir in the wind.

A gray pot, steam curling over the lip, sat next to him. Settled on the bottom, below the gray, salty water, a dozen cherrystone clams. He took one out, pried apart the already opening shell with a knife, made a quick cut, and offered it to me. I lifted the shell to my mouth and let the pink meat fall on my tongue—the feeling too slimy, the taste too salty, my mouth too full of the sea. He smiled as I grimaced, my shoulders trembling as I felt the clam sliding down into the deep pocket of my stomach.

I asked if I could push his button. Just before my finger touched the knot on the side of his head, he raised his hand and pressed it with his index finger. His mouth opened wide, his upper bridge dropping down against his bottom teeth, his mouth flashing silver and black. Dracula. For a moment his face calmed, shaped by something like pleasure, wonder. We both laughed.

I don't remember what happened to the rest of the clams, or when Dracula left the top step. It was a warm Saturday. I was eight or nine years old, and I walked from our rented house on the edge of an industrial park over to the monument sales office and sat down on the granite bench next to a dark gray gravestone. The grass was a brilliant green, the dogwood tree full of white blossoms. The wind picked up, the fir tree behind me shook, dappling the grass in front of my feet with sun and shadows. Sitting on the bench, listening to the birds, I followed the wind and sun and shadows as they slowly moved without the help of a clock. I experienced sensations—the smell of fir, the blink of a robin's eye, the gravestones spread across the lawn becoming buildings in a lush, green miniature city—and learned to wait for them without expectation.

Jorge Luis Borges once said that it is in the infinite that we encounter the beautiful (what Immanuel Kant called the sublime). I can look back on Dracula dropping his teeth countless times, forever be that boy sitting by his side. In his face I understood that even in the strangest, oddest moments there is beauty. Dracula smiled, looked at me without judgment or anger, elegant in black, an unharmed man. I think his name was Victor, though I will never know the truth of who he was, his story, his name. He had been in some accident or fight, some event he would never forget because every time he looked in the mirror he saw the damage. And every time I asked him if I could press his button, he waited for just the right moment and then lifted his tongue, pushed his bridge, and tasted memory.

Intervals

If I Were a Bell

My father in jeans, a chambray work shirt speckled with grease, tipping back the clear bottle of Miller, the beer gold, glistening, and downing the pony-sized beer in one long swallow. Eight ponies to a carton, short, fat bottles as if made for his hand, drunk so quickly, followed by a satisfied breath when he pulled the bottle from his lips as if he was trying to tell me, *There's nothing more perfect than a Saturday afternoon, working on a car, drinking cold beer, letting out a deep life breath.* The sweat dotting his shoulders and arms like ice. The champagne of beers, the high life, Miller Time in red script: memories of my father never yelling at me, never hitting me, always calling me *Freddie* in Spanish.

Why do people pick up and leave? What happened that caused my parents to flee from Connecticut to Michigan? For years I blamed my mother. My father drank too much, was surrounded by too many friends, his big family, and he wanted too often to be the life of the party. His fevered drinking along with his numbers selling became too unstable, risky, dangerous. My mother felt isolated, left out. Living among so many Puerto Ricans made her miss her own family. I got it all wrong. My mother was never to blame. Everything was my fault.

During the first grade I was often in trouble. I was hyperactive, couldn't stay on task, was disruptive in class, too expressive. School officials wanted to put me on Ritalin. This is the story I carried with me as my parents put me on a plane to Michigan. Once I arrived, I lived with my maternal grandparents, began first grade again with the hope that a new environment, a new school, and my grandfather's discipline would change me. The next summer when my parents drove out to Michigan to bring me home, I was so fat they hardly recognized me. *I don't eat that food*, I would say at the dinner table, and my grandfather would say, *Well, you do now–cause you ain't leaving the table till you do.* I sat at the table alone, the light outside beginning to fade. My grandfather turned off the light over the dining room table, me in the dark, night after night in front of a cold plate of food. I remember the gold square of light falling from the kitchen like a long curtain into the dining room, everything around me blue and gray shadows. Voices, laughter, the television flickering in the living room. Footfalls in the hall, closing doors, the quiet calm before sleep. I rocked in my chair, fought the drowsiness pushing my eyelids. My stomach grumbling. My grandfather took the plate away. *Go on to bed*, he said. The same plate the next night warm from the oven. I didn't want to be alone in the dark anymore. Wanted to watch television, listen to the talk and stories in the living room. I started to eat quickly, cleaned my plate fast.

I was still too expressive, still wild with energy, especially at school. One day at recess I hid below the small hill at the end of the playground. The end-of-recess bell had rung, and I stayed out in the cold wind, the ground a muddy gumbo, playing with fallen sticks and leaves. Eventually I got too cold, my feet wet and frozen, and I went inside covered in mud and was immediately sent to the principal's office. Suspended. My grandfather arrived with an old pair of shoes, took the new shoes he had recently bought for me that the principal had stuffed into a large manila envelope. At home, my grandfather's belt helped to slow me down, helped me to understand the expense of a ruined pair of shoes.

Back in Connecticut my parents had moved from Hartford to West Hartford so I could attend a better school, Charter Oak. I don't remember my father at home very much; he's working, he's out, he's somewhere in the city. I try to do better at school. Several times a week I'm sent down to a special class in the school's basement. Sitting in a chair next to a record player, wearing big, puffy headphones, a book spread across my lap as I read along with the voice on the record. I sit at a long table with a book filled with sentence-like lines, save there are no words; each sentence line is made of colorful objects and images: pine tree, orange, phone booth, red wagon. With a teacher at my side pointing at each image, I am to identify and pronounce each one—one after the other after the other, until a line, like a sentence, arrives at its conclusion. Sometimes there's math, sometimes there's drawing and painting, working with clay, but always there is the book with its sentences of objects and images. The pictograph of memory and learning.

I don't know what was wrong with me (pictograph, ideograph, *idiot*graph play in my mind in a continual loop). Why was I separated from the rest of the class? Why was I down in this basement classroom? Because I still encounter moments when my speech and pronunciation are troublesome, when the right English word doesn't appear in my mind, when the inflection and modulation of my voice are off, I assume there was something wrong with my speech. Something quite not right in how I expressed my learning. And I was supposedly hyperactive. No one has ever talked to me about that young boy, and when I let the images flash through my mind, I wonder if that is simply a boy I should forget.

Who's to say what happened back then? The psychodynamics of literacy and learning are so intimate, regardless of the social dimensions, that they can seem simple and ordinary; such an essential part of one's self, in fact, that they are easily taken for granted. It may have been that I was struggling with my bilingual life, and in my lack of linguistic ability to compose and articulate myself in an agreeable manner others saw a deficient and problematic student. Maybe. Maybe as I was listening to those two languages in my head, one would snap its fingers in time while the other began a melody on a piano, and for a moment I was a bell, a *cencerro*, filling with a song that needed its own special silence.

I am confused and ashamed by that time. How sad that in the first grade, my parents didn't know what to do with me and sent me away to Michigan. How sad that they brought me back home to Connecticut and a better school only for me to still struggle. I try to forget my temporary exile, even though it overshadows my childhood. And I have to forget: I was bad. Nothing wrong except I couldn't be good, I wasn't a calm, attentive, and agreeable boy at school.

A few years later we all moved to Michigan, where my parents lived a hard, sometimes poor life fraught with anger and pain as my father sank into alcoholism. Something in Michigan made his drinking worse. Would it have helped to ask, *Chago, is it my fault that we left Connecticut?* What good would it do to say, *Did the move to Michigan hurt you? Is it only through rage and silence that you can say you hate me?*

My father cannot speak of the past, cannot return to where our silence begins. What would it help to say, *Forgive me father for I have sinned . . . I never meant for you to forget.*

A bitter cold day. The classroom's windows are ice-frosted, outside, squares of bright blue sky above white swirling smoke. The radiator hisses. I'm moving from art station to art station, ruffling through sheets of construction paper, cutting strips with scissors, shaking pots of glue, acting a fool, acting as if I have come home drunk and the whole house needs to join me in the kitchen as I star in my one-man show, listen to what I say, look at me as I sit at the table knocking over glasses with my trembling hands. My classmates giggle, laugh, roll their eyes. The teacher tells me to settle down, get back to my station. More laughter, yelling. One group is making party streamers and horns. I grasp the small plastic whistle for the base of a horn and begin blowing, tooting, quacking—searching for every sound, loud, grating, screeching. The teacher jerks it from my mouth, yells to leave the room. She yells to go to the principal's office. I go, a flock of voices and languages fighting to follow me down the hall, and I'm suspended for the rest of the day.

When my mother drives me home I am too afraid to speak. From the corner of my eye I see her eyes fill with tears, watch them roll down the side of her face. The windshield fogs, the edges icy. My mother's hand turns red as she wipes a circle around the windshield, begins to scrape away the ice with her nails.

In my bedroom, cold light, the outline of my mother yellow and bright. She has my father's leather strap in her right hand. She tells me to undress. I cannot look at her hand, turn away as she strikes my bottom, strikes down along the back of my legs, my back, across my shoulders, the leather getting hotter, her arm and hand never tiring, my face smothered in tears.

Light has drained from the winter trees. The snow blues in the twilight. I find my mother at the kitchen table, the sewing machine's light casting a circle of gold over her hands as she coaxes a piece of material under the hammering needle she sets in motion with her foot. The needle stops. My mother bites off a piece of thread, looks at the finished hem. Her fingers run along the stiches.

I can't afford to take time from work. I can get in trouble for leaving—I want to say these are her words as she turns off her sewing machine, the circle of light suddenly gone. Whatever her words, I remember what was most important: my mother was losing money, was jeopardizing her job and helping me to remember the fire of leather, my burning shoulders.

Forever branded: How can I ever forget the sensations of class.

My mother is working on a pattern. She has scissors, her sewing machine, the pattern laid out on the kitchen table, and in the middle a cloth pincushion that resembles a plump tomato with green leaves. It's winter, we're now living in Michigan, on Day Street, my mother is not working and it's a snow day. No school, too cold to go outside, nothing to do but sit by the frozen picture window, scrape away a circle, watch the trains pass on the tracks out front as they head west to Chicago or pull into the station a block away from our apartment. Steam rising from the engines, snow falling and mixing with the steam, the sound of the crossing alarm before the viaduct, the train's turning wheels grinding against steel, intervals of silence, steam, the cold blue sky. My mother is leaning close to the pattern, cutting fabric, several pins sticking out between her lips. *Here, I'll bring the light closer*, I say, and grab the brass ring on the bottom of the lamp hanging from the ceiling. *No*, my mother tries to yell, and it's too late because I'm pulling hard on the brass ring, the wires crackling, snapping, sparks shooting overhead, and the room goes dark as the lamp crashes on the table. I try to run away but my mother catches me just as I touch my bedroom door. She beats me with her hand, grabs my belt, strikes my shoulders and arms as I cry on my bed, let the fiery leather take me to sleep.

My mother is still working on her pattern. Her father is leaning over the table, winding electrical tape around the frayed wires. The lamp was too old to pull down before, but now it works good as new, and looking down at the table I follow the black lines, the numbers and circles of my mother's pattern. The crinkled tan tissue paper,

the shapes like streets and lakes, rail lines and highways and bound-
aries, an old map I try to quickly memorize before its secret routes
are forever lost.

*
* *

There are still a few small scars on my back. When I raise my shoulders, run my fingertips along them, I feel a faint calligraphy—lines
like broken twigs or fine stiches—feel again the striking leather. This
slow disappearance makes room for memory.

I'm four or five, standing on a kitchen chair. Back in Connecticut
in one of our small apartments. On top of the white refrigerator is
a porcelain percolator patterned with blue flowers I can softly feel
with my fingertips. I want to help. I turn, see my parents sitting at
the table with cups of coffee, and they look up. Smile. Maybe someone yells, *No*. Maybe someone yells, *Freddie*. Maybe someone stands
up, a chair falling against the floor. My hands touching the porcelain, smooth, warm. The outlines of the raised blue flowers. When
I lift the pot the porcelain is hot, scalding coffee pouring down my
neck, over my stomach, across my shoulders, down my back. The
smell of coffee burning my skin.

Only coffee. Cup after cup, hot, black, no sugar. A flash of white:
the large gauze bandage taped across my chest and stomach. A
policeman standing in the hall. My mother and father at my side
as I'm wheeled on a gurney down a glaring corridor, feeling heat
rise along my shoulder blades, the skin of my stomach dry and stiff
and still on fire.

An ox lumbering in a field, sweat on his skin, red dust powdering his hooves. The heat of the leather strikes my shoulders. I
touch the ox's flank. We steady each other, step by step, making
our way across a cane field, the sun—like memory—falling on our
backs.

*
**

Intervals. Now and then. Here and there. I still struggle with the pronunciation of words, the blank spot in my mind as I search for the right word. The inability to be around a group of people for too long (I'm too silent, too often at the edge of the conversation, oddly self-exiled, must have something up my sleeve). I have a PhD in English, and no matter all the years I've offered to reading and writing I still possess a piss-poor vocabulary. I've come up with a new plan; every day take one word I've encountered, a word I've seen or heard out in the world, a word I've read in a book, a word remembered from a dream, and then as I write I try to discover that word's life. My hope is to expand my vocabulary, build one word onto another, my words lifting my voice to radiant new heights.

The word today is *interval*, found in *The Autobiography of William Carlos Williams*. He writes of intervals and "intervals of thought," the intervals of winter and spring, and the intervals of doctoring and writing. As in a space between things or points or selves, a space of time as well, a space that might exist without time too, as in the different pitches between tones. Intervals creating juxtaposition and motion and rhythm and space and shape and music. Memory, too, as theme and variation arise from within to create spots of time patterned into recollections. As in the pain of a leather belt is all the more memorable because of the interval of a raised arm, a hand momentarily stilled, and then the waiting for the return of the belt, the sudden striking fire. Or, better yet, the interval between bell and *cencerro*, pausing within the space and pitch between two languages, as in tapping a bell and *tocando el cencerro*, if only to then become the bell, *cencerro*, tied around the neck of an ox, filling with the clomping of his hooves, clanging alongside the sugarcane swaying in the breeze as he pulls a heavily loaded wagon up a dirt road, its wheels turning red in the twilight.

Roytype

My father undressed on the back porch. I stood in the dark kitchen
and watched. Moonlight poured through the windows. Suspended
above the tall beech tree the moon was a pool of silver light. My
father's skin smooth like the underbelly of a fish, his arms looking
bruised, and when he dropped his navy blue uniform shirt with
his name over the left pocket, his torso gleamed and revealed the
ink stains from work, a faint watermark running along his ribs. He
pulled a typewriter ribbon from his pants and held the spool up to
the moonlight as if it were a monocle or a telescope. He swayed,
the outline of his body beginning to blur, and lay the ribbon on a
windowsill. I stepped onto the porch, took my father's hand, and
led him through the unlit kitchen to the couch in the living room.
He sat on the edge of the couch for a moment, looked at his shaking hands, and then tucked them under his arms as he lay down.
I spread a blanket over him. Lying on the carpet, my back against
the bottom of the couch, I covered myself with the hanging bit of
blanket, the rug scratchy against my ribs as I shivered. When I was
younger my mother and my father's brother Ismael would watch

old black-and-white movies on Friday nights. They drank from short red glasses, and the faceted glass on the sides reflected the flicker of the TV as a horse took off and a cloud of dust took over the screen, or as a woman and a man kissed for so long, their faces big and white, that I thought they might just slide off the screen and roll across the living room floor. Ismael would always ask, a small smile starting his words as he pointed at the door behind us, *What will you do when your papa walks in?* Those words always made me feel as if Ismael and my mother were not watching the movie, those red glasses with their mysterious liquid never existed, and the only reason we were gathered there on Friday evenings was to wait for my father. I had a little plastic hammer in my hand, curled up in a chair or sometimes sitting cross-legged on the floor, the orange hammer head against my palm as I gripped the blue handle, and then I would strike the air (or sometimes my palm) violently five or six whacks, saying in a loud, happy voice, *I'm going to hit him over the head—pow pow pow—and tell him to get to bed.* A commercial played during these brief exchanges, the sparkling, winking eye of Mr. Clean or the jingle *Sometimes you feel like a nut, sometime you don't* or *Plop, plop, fizz, fizz, oh what a relief it is.* My mother and uncle always laughed when I said that, though their eyes never seemed to leave the TV, and in that flickering light I see the outline of my head turned toward the screen and wonder what's so funny, and why am I so loud and happy when I imagine my father walking through the door, perhaps swaying a bit, smelling strongly of rum and cigarettes, looking elegant in his work uniform, the sleeves rolled tight above his elbows, as I leap from behind and strike him over the head with that little plastic hammer. Back in that living room, now Saturday morning, back there in those memories that return to me without my understanding, I wake up on the couch with the blanket tucked up under my neck. I smell coffee, hear my father singing in a low, sweet voice, and then he's crinkling open a package of crackers, and

I know he'll probably cut some wedges of gouda cheese and slices of guava paste from a tin for breakfast. I lift my hand from under the blanket, turn it above my eyes, the back dotted and smeared by my father's purple fingerprints, and lying next to me are the typewriter ribbon and my hammer. Sometimes I think I'm only remembering a dream, and yet there are times when my hand tingles and burns with something quick and hard and brighter than the moon will ever be.

World on a String

My father owned a fat cone of blue string. It had a short red pole in the center, and wound around the pole were thousands and thousands of feet of string. He pulled long pieces across his garden, tied them to wooden stakes, and made his bean, pepper, and tomato rows perfectly straight. It usually sat on a shelf in a tool cabinet on the back porch, or on the kitchen counter. It never seemed to lose any of its size, as if the cone had some secret for lasting forever. I knew not to play with it, though I sometimes cut off pieces to join soldiers, link a truck and a jeep, or string together some punched papers to keep them in order.

One Saturday morning he brought out a kite, maybe two feet in length, made of a red plastic sheet and a cross of light, thin wood, and for its tail a strip of yellow cloth knotted in three places. He took me across the avenue to the asphalt field, and we walked to the middle where the weeds broke through in thin islands of green and the asphalt was a wide black-and-gray sea. The wind rushed in our ears. He tied the string to the kite. Walking backward, the cone tucked under his arm like a loaf of bread, my father let out the string while

I held on to the kite. Once he was about twenty feet away he nodded, and I ran toward him as fast as I could, the kite raised over my head as if I were about to throw a paper airplane, and when he yelled, *Let go!* I released it, let it lift into the wind, watched the red diamond shudder and then slowly rise, its yellow tail dancing behind it. My father leaned back, let the string continue to escape from his cone, one twisting blue arc after another. I followed the string up until it disappeared, then followed the silent space to the kite as it rose higher and higher, became smaller and smaller.

The wind continued to roar, the kite rose, and when my father handed me the cone, I tucked it under my arm, held the string in my hand, my index finger curving around the line pulsating in the wind, the blue sky: my heart raced for all the weight the string lifted and held so high.

"The creative life!" Henry Miller exclaims. Then, "Ascension. Passing beyond oneself. Rocketing out into the blue, grasping at flying ladders, mounting, soaring, lifting the world up by the scalp, rousing the angels from their ethereal lairs, drowning in stellar depths, clinging to the tails of comets." Makes my scalp tingle. A cold breeze rising on my arms. My fingers shaking. Not me feeling the creative life through the kite's lifting and soaring onto its solitary path—no, not me, not me at all. I remember my father—for that one brief moment—sharing his creative life. He had felt the wind that morning, imagined a kite, made it for me, saw how his blue string could make it more than memory. For once he wasn't short with me, silent, in a hurry to be somewhere—anywhere—else. The sky grew brighter, the wind blew colder, and we let the kite rise higher and higher. When it became an *A* smudged with thin clouds, so high only angels could have written the letter, my father took his knife and cut the string, and the kite began to swerve and dip and rise on its own, to fly to wherever it needed to go, a red-and-yellow diamond to some, the *A* now a yellow-and-red seahorse to me, galloping above the city, heading out over the Atlantic.

My father's friend pulled into the driveway with a new used car. Soon there would be a light hanging inside its raised hood, tools glinting on fenders. Beer to drink. Stories and laughter and memory. Maybe later some Canadian whiskey. My father walked away, his knife tucked into his belt, his cone of blue string cradled in his elbow.

In the backyard my father's string stretched across his garden, held up his bean, pepper, and tomato plants, helping them grow taller and greener, helping them to stand straight. I stood between a row of plants, listened as they swayed in the wind, felt the string thrumming against my palm, and though I didn't say it aloud, I dared them to rise so they might feel what it's like to gallop in blue fields from cloud to cloud to cloud.

Peppers

My father had driven out to the airport to pick up his younger brother Ché, who was arriving for the first time from Puerto Rico. His brothers Eddie and Ismael were also in the car. They, too, had followed my father to Hartford; as the oldest brother, he helped them find work. Headed back to the city they passed around a bottle of rum and laughed. The windows were cracked open, and their cigarette smoke drifted in the headlights of the oncoming cars before winding out the windows. My father took a long drink, listened to his swallows. Only after he let out a deep breath did he hear Ché's shaking voice, hear his name over and over and over, *Cha-ging, Cha-ging, Cha-ging.* He pulled to the side of the road and switched on the overhead light. In the backseat Ché had a cassette case opened on his lap. He raised his head, looked at my father, and held out handfuls of money, his hands trembling as if the bills burned his fingers.

Imagine the inside of the terminal: the rows of blue plastic seats, the scattered newspapers, the empty coffee cups, and there under the edge of a magazine the brown cassette case. Ché had never stolen a thing in his life, not even a pack of gum or a mango from a stranger's tree. That fraction of a second, excited and happy to see his brothers, warm from their embraces, Ché, fresh off the plane, grabbed what seemed—sitting there alone on a seat—a gift of welcome. I can still hear Ché's shaking voice, feel the cold air on my face slipping through the car's open windows, swirling with wonder and promise, and see my father's smile.

*
**

My father begins his story again. We are eating dinner, bowls of rice with red beans in front of us, a dish of steaming chicken in the middle of the table, the pieces pepper flecked. Next to my father's plate is a glass of water and a short bottle filled with small yellow, green, and orange peppers floating in vinegar and pineapple juice, salt and pepper, bits of garlic. My father pauses, takes a long drink of water. Sprinkles the pepper sauce over his plate. Eats a few spoonfuls. Once again he repeats his name three times, becomes Ché, his arms and shoulders shaking as he holds out his empty, trembling hands. He laughs, picks up his spoon. More than $1,500. It's incredible, he says. He mentions the numbers, the Mafia. There was no one around. All that money sitting there for free.

Sometimes at dinner he became talkative. Mostly his face was turned down, his spoon quickly raised to his mouth, his plate clean in four or five minutes. He'd get the hiccups. Leave the table, head out back to tend to his garden or work on a car. There were times he ate slowly, looked around, told stories of his dreams, fantastic events, seahorses as tall as our refrigerator galloping on the waves of the Caribbean. And always stories of work.

Sometimes the hot pepper sauce was in a pint bottle of rum, and I knew then it was homemade, given to my father from someone who had recently returned from the island. Sometimes I found peppers tucked under the skin of a chicken leg, deep in the red sauce of beans, hiding at the bottom of my rice. I might be laughing at something he said, my mouth full of food. Or more than likely quiet—the whole table quiet—my father bent over his plate. My mouth suddenly tingled with heat, and then it grew as if a match had been struck on the back of my tongue. Searing, hot pain, my eyes beginning to tear. I drained my water only for the heat to soar, scorching. My father stopped eating, sat there with the biggest smile, started laughing, his eyes wrinkled, his cheeks flushed. He didn't seem to do this out of meanness. He really thought it was funny. I accepted it because anything was better than his silence. He was never much of a talker, but he could express his rage easily, his knuckles quickly striking the top of my head. The peppers hidden in my food were meant to say: *I care for you. I am thinking of you. Never, never waste a bowl of rice.*

I learned to wait for this loving pain. Wondered where it might be hidden, waited to feel the rising heat, followed his eyes and mouth and hands. Often, nothing happened. Then, as he sat there quietly, I wished he'd say anything.

My father scrapes the last pearls of rice from his bowl. There is no conclusion to this story. If there's a purpose, it's only to remind me that money will never be mine to find.

I close my eyes, remember my father at the table, and wait for his voice. I listen to it like the rhythm of my breath—breathing in, breathing out—gulping air as I try to cool the fire beginning to burn.

Patina

My father had found another apartment in the city. Once a redbrick liquor store. He and my mother made a deal with the landlord to turn it into a small apartment, and in return the rent was reduced. A first memory: four years old, crouched down so low my butt touches the back of my heels. I'm wearing tan shorts and a dark brown shirt with colored stripes, and wide rays of sunlight surround me, float me in a light-filled sea. My sandy blond hair, my serious face, my shoulders cool on cement as I look up at Lafayette—the Marquis de Lafayette—riding his verdigris horse. My eyes follow the underside of his mouth, his thick, muscular neck, and the leather reins that pull his bridle's bit, his tongue thick between sharp teeth. *Marie Joseph Paul de Lafayette*, b. 1757, stilled forever on this small island of grass and concrete on the corner of Capital Avenue and Lafayette Street, summer of 1969 or '70, Hartford, Connecticut. The horse sweating, the clomp-clomp-clomp of his hooves like a palm striking a conga drum as he trots the Marquis into battle, sword held high into an empty blue sky. Childhood: Möbius strip of tearing down walls, painting, cleaning, the smell of bleach and oranges moving from one apartment to another. My mother's hair and hands powdered with white dust, broken boards and pieces of plaster balanced on her arms. Standing in a doorway as summer light streams behind her glinting with copper motes. And my father, one hand holding a hammer and the other a beer, always trying to clench the strip together. The trees sway in the breeze, leaf shadows dappling concrete, my arms awash in cool, wet blue-green. Where—boy who I once was—where, I need to ask, does memory begin, where does it end? Why can I still taste this chalky, steely sweat as I lick my palm after holding the horse's hoof and wait for my mother and father to call me so I can charge into the rest of my life?

Newfoundland

My father stands behind his white Dodge van. He wears black pants, shirtless, his forearm leaning against the back door. He has a small belly, his biceps are firm, his nipples rosy brown, and down the middle of his chest a row of hair. The summer sun has darkened his skin. His smile is genuine, joyful, as if he had just been laughing. A simple snapshot taken with my mother's black-and-silver pocket Kodak. The tones are a heavy gold, and the composition is almost perfect. He's wearing his pith helmet tipped back on his head, and a curly lock of hair falls on his forehead.

On that morning, a car—a powder blue Volkswagen Bug—passed quickly, hit a curve, and swerved, its tires squealing, and then flipped on its side. My father dropped his dripping rag into the bucket. He turned toward the street. The passenger door opened, and a thick head of hair rose up. The driver lifted himself through the doorway, swung his legs over the edge, and dropped down. He looked at my father and me, punched the tire, and yelled. He walked around the underside. Slowly the car started to rock, back and forth, more quickly, until it lifted, the space between the Bug and the street growing, as it teetered in the air. With one hard push it was upright on its wheels. The man jumped inside, started it, and was quickly on his way, grinning at us through the cracked windshield.

My father stood on the curb. He stepped forward. He waved his pith helmet as the man sped away.

My mother stood on the corner. She held a small cooler, and tucked underneath her arm a plaid blanket. When my father turned, he couldn't stop grinning, and his face seemed to ask, *Did you see that?* He leaned against the back of his van. Around my mother's wrist was the strap of her camera. She raised it to her right eye. Her left eye wrinkled like a star.

My father was never one to stay home on weekends. He always had someplace to go. He drove to the mountains and streams of New Hampshire and Vermont, along the shore in Connecticut, or up to Boston or west to New York. On that morning he drove north for hours through the woods. Sitting in the back of his van, I turned and looked through the back windows: an endless blue sky, the tops of green trees, and, below, the black road with its yellow center line like a long, brightly patterned slithering snake. The pine and birch trees shuffled together, sunlight and shadows mixed, the flash of a silver stream breaking through the trees. The van slowed down. My father pulled to the side of the road. Two women were approaching, each carrying a tall backpack with a rolled sleeping bag tied to the top. The side door slid open and they hoisted their packs into the van, stepped inside, and closed the door. They seemed to collapse on the floor. One woman wore cut-off jeans, and a white strip of skin showed between the bottom of her jeans and her tanned thigh. The other woman looked deeply asleep, lying on her side, her face turned toward me, and her chest rose high with her breaths. At the edge of her T-shirt I could see her clavicle and a red lace bra strap across her shoulder. I was lying on the backseat looking down on them, the van beginning to cool as the sun moved away from the road, the back of the van filling with streams of light sparkling with dust motes, the shadows from the woods we passed falling through the windows. Her eyes opened. She spread her arms. I slipped off the backseat and lay next to her. She held me close. Her arms were soft and warm, and the light rhythm of her breathing helped me to fall asleep.

When I awoke the women stood in the grass, their backpacks leaning against their legs. My father lifted the engine cover. My mother handed him the plaid blanket. When he shut off the engine the carburetor popped, and bright, jagged flames rose inside the van, my father beating them down with the blanket. The heat crawled up my arms, the sharp smell of oil and gas and burning wool filling my nose and throat, the blanket ends sparking. The women thanked my parents for the ride. They walked away. Their backpacks and legs slowly became smaller on the road—thick dark woods on one side, a sandy beach and the ocean on the other. The road curved, they disappeared and continued on to Newfoundland.

"Childhood memories often consist of small, trivial details that come from nowhere," the novelist Patrick Modiano writes. Soon my parents moved from the old liquor store apartment to 85 Reed Avenue, where, on the edge of an industrial park, they rented the small white house next to the monument sales office. A house just over Hartford's border and barely within the town limits of West Hartford. Away from my father's family, the parties, the swirling sounds and streets and people of Little Puerto Rico—85 Reed Avenue may have provided moments, perhaps days, when my mother found the distance she needed. And there was a new chance for me at school, too, since I had trouble learning in the city, was disruptive and hyperactive, moving back and forth between Spanish and

English. But first my parents took me to the airport and I was sent away to Michigan. When my parents picked me up a year later and drove me back to Connecticut, I saw the house on Reed Avenue for the first time.

The house looked vacant, the yard empty, the front porch bare, and the picture window without curtains. Aside from the loading docks and trucks, it seemed as if we were living on an abandoned corner, in a neighborhood in a different country, a different time. When I stood in the front yard by the catalpa tree in the twilight and looked across the fields toward Hartford the tenements seemed miles away, and when their windows flashed I saw the lights on a ship floating in the darkening sea.

The sun began to set, burnishing the Atlantic in gold, and my father led us on a wooden walkway across a cranberry bog and over some short dunes. The trees along the bog were still green with leaves, and when the wind blew through them, like lifting a blanket into the air before you let it fall and spread out on the sand, it got colder and I ran toward the beach. To the north stars began to shine in the deep blue sky.

At the age of eighteen I returned to Hartford from Michigan. In three days I found three jobs—working the night shift at a donut shop, stocking and bagging groceries at a market during the day, and on Tuesday evenings and Saturdays and Sundays I pumped gas at a station on New Britain Avenue. Some days I was lucky to get four or five hours' sleep, and I often took a brief nap between 7:00 and 9:00 a.m. or during my lunch break. My body became numb, I suffered from bouts of dizziness, and my hands always felt sore, as if invisible pins were sticking my palms and fingertips. "The unseen design of things is more harmonious than the seen," Heraclitus wrote. I rented an apartment across the street from the Bushnell Theatre, and every day as I walked to and from work I passed Lafayette's statue. I weighed 250 pounds when I arrived, but in less than

9 months dropped to 145. It was as if inside me I carried a long lost self that had finally returned. I quit working at the donut shop but kept the other two jobs. I had more time to walk the streets, stop somewhere for a drink, or simply come home and sit by the window and watch the twilight move down the fire escape steps. I was often hungry, wanted to see how far I could go on a cup of coffee, was lightheaded, and yet every day was grand because I was feasting on memory in the neighborhood of childhood.

Nineteen, maybe twenty, I come across an old white farmhouse with a red-shingled roof. So many acres with a stream that runs all the way to the Atlantic, and in the fall you can catch migrating salmon on your own land. Eighty thousand dollars seems like a steal. There used to be a magazine feature, perhaps in *Esquire* or *Outside*, a small paragraph of text with an equally small drawing or photograph to accompany it. Each described an out-of-the-way and overlooked place, often rural and cheap, and I imagined this feature was for rich people looking for a second home. That white farm-house in Newfoundland was a home I knew I could live in forever. It had a screened-in porch, and I could see a couple of wood chairs and a blueberry crate turned on its side with a book and a dark drink resting on top. It's twilight. The stream gurgles in the bluing light drifting through the fir trees and filling the field, and after a long day of work all I want to do is watch the fireflies light up over the tall canary grass. Think of getting a goat or an ox or a horse to graze in the field. I cut out the paragraph and image and carried it in my wallet for a decade. There would be some unexpected change or breakthrough in my life—like money falling from the sky—and I would buy that farmhouse. The piece of paper became creased to knifelike edges over the years, and the print smudged along the edges and bled through the glossy paper. I could still see the house and price clearly. When the clipping finally split in half, though, I threw it away. I'd never saved $80,000 anyway, and never even made half that much in a year.

Back in the 1970s, when moving was such a simple and necessary fact of life, I stood in the sand between a cranberry bog and the ocean. I followed a blue heron flying straighter and faster across the sky. I walked toward the shore. Sea grass trembled in the wind, turned blue-green as the sunlight weakened along the Atlantic, and sea sounds surrounded my steps. I turned back. My father stood on the walkway, leaned against the handrail as the shadows spread along the beach. He waved his pith helmet wildly over his head.

There are things I carry within that I still can't name. My father's van, his spirit for the road, his travel and work. Dreams. Memories. A country I still don't know. I am left with one word. Some days I repeat it over and over again, as if it's something I might call my own.

How My Father Taught Me to Write

My father never owned a typewriter. Still, he would often bring home typewriter ribbons in his black metal lunchbox. I found the red-and-black ribbons intriguing, special, the way they were split down the middle perfectly: half red, half black. (Those long roads I imagined and made: I wanted to follow them to unknown places, my dreams still not deadened by tired muscles, bruised ribs, hands numb from working in fields or a factory or a gas station to earn the money needed to get me down those red-and-black roads.)

It is summer. I'm maybe nine and choosing not to read this late afternoon, I'm trying to learn to write, unaware that I'm inhabiting a moment of self-invention. I sit at a picnic table under the tall beech tree. I have a blank piece of paper in front of me with a strip of ribbon spread across it. Holding a pencil stub I press letters into the ribbon, but no matter how hard I press, no color or ink or letters appear. There are faint spots, the outline of letters like the pattern left on your windshield by an unlucky moth on a darkening road. I keep trying, harder, wet the tip of my pencil with my tongue, willing the wings to be whole. When I slowly lift the ribbon invisible words stand there, little squares or circles of objects or parts of my mind impressed in the white, and then they join together as sentences slowly unfurl across the azure sea behind my eyes, and in the back of my ears they begin to sound like waves, music, friendship, forever. *This beech tree is tall. The garden is growing. When we fish along the New London seashore the flat flounders swim under our boat. Chago is what I call my father whose ribbons make these words. The sky is its own sea of blue and white drifting above this tree. In the fall, a hurricane hummed in its leaves in the pink early morning light, and my soldiers were nowhere in sight.* At 5:00 p.m. workers would rush out of Roytype like a blue wave, like a flag snapping in the wind, like men in a parade who owned the street—talking, laughing, suddenly alive as they untucked their shirts, took them off and wiped their backs, shook hands, waved good-bye with their lunchboxes or thermoses or rolled-up newspapers, and broke off into groups or alone for cars and bus stops or liquor stores and taverns.

My father always stood out to me in his blues, something dignified and proud about the uniform no matter how hard the work may have been. Over his left pocket, over his heart, there was an oval patch stitched to his shirt, and in cursive in that oval the name *Chuck.* Because I had always called my father Chago, I saw Chuck as my father's other name, his English name, since in my childhood mind Chago and Chuck were not that far apart.

Over time his navy blue uniforms began to fade and soften with washings, as if draining of ink, and sometimes on Fridays my father would arrive in the middle of the night drunk, and as he undressed on the back porch or in the kitchen, when moonlight fell onto his body, I saw his underwear streaked with blue and gray, and along his forearms and thighs there were purple stripes.

***

In the morning light a shirt draped over a chair, the stitching on the oval frayed and broken, the cursive name flipped over and unreadable.

My father never gave me many words (they clung to his silence, and that silence had its own special color—a deep blood red sometimes, a blackened bruise of blue others). Some broken English, some fragmented Spanish is what I received, and although these words were mostly housed in his angry yelling, I searched in the silences for other tones and colors I might faintly hear. He never offered or explained his name, Chago, though it was all I ever knew and called him. Never father, dad, papa, or papi.

It would be years before I learned my father's full name, and then I felt a loss because I had not been like other boys who did not call their fathers by name. I never learned what my father did at Roytype, and now I remember his working simply because he brought those ribbons home, and without any verbal meaning they became essential to my personal alphabet. They helped me to touch words.

From spools I pull ribbons that become colorful bandages for my G.I. Joes, or very long victory flags for my imagined battle scenes. Ribbons form tents of canvas over wood scraps and become a shelter for a jeep in a desert. I unfurl ribbons across the linoleum floor and they become long roads. The back porch windows shake, I listen to the winter wind pushing against the house and picture the waves rushing in, crashing white, swelling fat and gray-blue on Ocean Beach. I tear the piece of paper in half and then fold each half into a neat bundle. One is stuffed deep into Joe's khaki shirt, tucked there along his ribs, and the other is packed into the back of his jeep.

The cold floor, the creaking windows, the shadow of the beech tree swaying in the thickening dusk, those unfurled ribbons, those bundles—secret messages that someone else will need to read.

In my late thirties, trying to become a writer whose words could take hold with permanence to the page, I began to hunger for the attention I brought to those words that never appeared as I pressed a pencil against a typewriter ribbon. It is the attention I will need to reveal their secrets, to discover all the ink and color and tones in *Chago*, how underneath his work uniform script of *Chuck*, floating on its own sea over his heart, there is a name I still need to touch and learn to write: Santiago. Not Saint James. Not Iago. Not only Chago and Chuck but also *Santiago* typed forever across my ribbon of memory.

Like a Thief in the Night

Some nights I want to cut a circle around the top of my skull, open it, peer inside, follow the red and blue lines, the edges of smeared letters or shadows, until a dim street sign appears on a corner and marks the only neighborhood I ever had. The gate is wide open, and if not, I ooze over that pink wall of brain and blood, liquid-like, and drop down onto 85 Reed Avenue. The monument sales office. The Columbia Music Hall. The small red house on the banks of the brook. Mr. Donut. In the distance the Hartford tenements. The UPS terminal. The passing trucks heading in and out of the industrial park, to and from destinations I'll never know. The light and shadows along the grass of the mock graveyard. Not quite a neighborhood, bounded on all sides by work, only a handful of houses, no childhood friends. A past filled with the rising dust of trucks, the smell of hot asphalt, the sun caught in the trees making everything glow, and as I look through the dust and sunlight I see a boy standing under a catalpa tree.

Across the street he gathered clover for his rabbits, ran across the long field of asphalt and concrete, the tall grass and weeds scratching the undersides of his outstretched arms. A boy riding his bike up and down the thin black road running through the grave-yard. A boy gathering ticket stubs from the parking lot of the music hall. A boy climbing over a stockade fence and, on the other side, walking and counting the different tones of rust collecting on tools and machinery glinting in the jumbled lumber and steel. A boy watching the wind drop the dry leaves and hard pods of the catalpa tree to the ground, and then waiting for the moon to rise, waiting for its cold light to fall on his hands as he sits on a stone bench next to a gravestone. Snow falling through a tree, and he's still stand-ing at the window looking at the outline that had once shaped a man, his father, passed out in the snow. White blossoms, spring, a man called Dracula sitting on the top step of the front porch with a pot of steaming cherrystone clams at his side, his black leather driving gloves folded on his thigh. Out in the driveway a car up on blocks, a silver lamp hanging from its raised hood, the clink of a dropped wrench striking gravel. In the late afternoon backyard—the picnic table covered with bowls and platters and plates, the smell of roasted pork and achiote and cilantro, the melody of a strummed guitar escaping from an open window.

Now, years gone, standing in the future, I try to keep my mind focused, alone in the present, holding close the particulars at hand—the gold lamplight warming the tabletop, the soft thrumming of cars out on the highway heading east or west, a half glass of brandy the night's fragrant perfume—memories like grass and weeds and purple clover break through. I listen to the voices speaking and laughing and crying in a language of what must have been. Hear the broken phrases out in the backyard, try to understand the words before they disappear. On the edge of a neighborhood that's so small you can barely find it on a map. Once again I climb over the wall, steal back what was once mine, fold it up, put it away, because only I can carry it tonight.

Part II
MICHIGAN

Sometimes it's not possible to remember exactly what happened during a certain phase of your life, a certain season, to remember what you did or said at the time, who you said it to, remember the weekdays, the schooldays and birthdays, who was invited and how many years they carried with them, but you do remember what colours the days were, and your palms remember the soft, the smooth, and the rough, remember every surface, remember stones and the bark of trees, remember water, and you remember a piece of clothing, that it was important, but not why it was important, and you suddenly remember a telephone number, but you don't remember who it was that you were calling, 25 00 45, who could that have been, and a sentence comes to mind, but you can't remember if it was him or you who said it, but it didn't matter, for no one could tell your voices apart. But you can remember what the weather was like, and the sky above, all the skies, and all the days had the same sign, it was plus, plus, plus, and they came towards you and passed by in slow motion . . .

—PER PETTERSON, I REFUSE

Trash Truck

We were gathered around the kitchen table looking into a cardboard box. Inside there was a wilting head of lettuce, a loaf of sandwich bread, two cartons of orange juice, a bag of dusty-looking potatoes, a half-gallon of milk, and an onion with black splotches. My father took out a carton of juice. Sunlight fell through the window glass covered with amorphous lines and shapes, as if clouds or frozen lakes had been etched into the panes. My mother and younger sister—six years old to my ten—stood next to my father, their faces still, their arms held close to their sides, the wind throwing small pieces of sharp snow against the window. My father shook the carton of orange juice and set it down on the table. He pushed back the top and broke open the carton's mouth. He poured juice into four glasses. I'm watching his hand lift a glass, and then it's my hand grasping and lifting a glass to my mouth: cold, pulpy, sweeter than any juice I've tasted. My father's face never betrayed an emotion, save that he was the angriest man in the world. I can't tell if he likes or hates this juice. My mother and sister lift their glasses. No one says a word. We stand in that faded light and listen to each other swallow.

Before my father had the opportunity to move to Chicago and try to sober up, he had the desire to become a trash man. Many families in our town kept fifty-five-gallon barrels in their yards to burn their trash. It was fascinating and disgusting to watch a plastic bag slowly tear and break apart because of the crumpled piece of newspaper I had lit with a match and dropped into the barrel. I listened to the paper crackle, smelled the putrid plastic and aluminum and eggshells and coffee grounds beginning to burn, a funnel of gray and black smoke rising from the barrel. As a trash man my father went around town and dumped the full barrels of ashes into the back of his pickup, spread them with a pitchfork and shovel as they grew higher, and once his truck could hold no more, he drove the ashes to the dump and shoveled them out. It was cold, hard, honest work.

My father always had small dreams. If only he could come into enough money so he wouldn't have to work a full-time job. Who knows, maybe he could one day make enough to return to the island paradise of Puerto Rico and live like a king. There was the hope of winning the numbers or the lottery. There was the extra money he made selling the numbers in Connecticut. There was the old utility van that he was going to fix up with a fridge, stove, and freezer. Out on the streets of Hartford he'd sell *pinchos, papas rellenas, alcapureos, piraguas*, and ice cream as warm music—salsa, boleros, perhaps a *danza*—escaped from his van. There were the old tires on rims and the cans of red and white paint. Working from the memory of a planter he had seen, he cut triangles into the tires, like a row of sharp diamonds around the edge of the rim, and pulled the tire inside out, breaking the diamonds free. He painted each diamond in a pattern of red, white, red, white, and then painted the rest in wide bands, filled it with soil, and planted hostas. He lined his planters up underneath the catalpa tree in our front yard and waited for someone to drive by, see them, and stop to buy one for $7.50.

What was it about living in Michigan, our family, and his life that sparked in his imagination the possibility of making money with a trash truck? Why did he want to shovel those ashes, flip them up into the air, and breathe that gray and black and white ash? What was it that made him think we would want to drink expired milk and orange juice, eat old lettuce and potatoes and onions he had found behind a grocery store?

We had moved from Connecticut to Michigan a few years before. Both my mother and father had a difficult time finding work, and for a time they picked apples and were on welfare. The new car my father had brought from Connecticut was repossessed. I don't remember going hungry, and clothes from Goodwill or a garage sale never hurt me. My mother had worked for Bell Telephone Company and a transfer wasn't yet available. Her father gave us an apartment to live in, then at the end of the fall he gave us another, and maybe I never understood what was going on: my parents never rented these apartments because my grandfather let us stay there for free.

My father's trash truck was a beautiful deep turquoise green, a late 1960s or early '70s pickup with a white grill. The long bench seat wide and hard, the square dash with its bright instruments and their big numbers and lines, the shiny heat vents, and the radio's knobs and buttons like mirrors in the winter light. He drove down the back drive behind Peele's Grocery. There were empty milk racks by the loading dock, some broken pallets, a rusty dumpster. He stopped, put the truck in Park, and we opened our doors and almost ran up to the dock. There was a waxed cardboard lettuce box filled with cartons of orange juice, some dented cans without labels, wilting lettuce and celery, and a few red-and-white cartons of milk. We each took a side, lifted it from the dock, and carried the box back to the truck.

*
**

This is what I know of my father's life. At the age of eight or nine, in the third grade, my father's father made him quit school to begin working. Every summer, when the heat soared in Puerto Rico, my abuelo came to Connecticut to work out on the turnpike at Coach's Grill. So it was only natural that at the age of seventeen my father would follow in his father's footsteps. But now, on the mainland, my father moves toward his own choices and decides, once the summer has ended, not to return to the island. A few years later he migrates to Michigan for work in a Green Giant mushroom cannery, and one evening he meets my mother, who's still attending high school. My father is four years older than my mother. The first time he brings her home her father is waiting in the yard with a shotgun. My father might as well be from a different country, and yet he and my mother have fallen in love. My mother quits high school so they can marry. Soon I'm born.

There's so much of his life I'll never know. To even understand his life I might have to imagine it, and thus make my father the hero of a novel I might title *A Minor Life*, *A Lesser Life*, or *Epigraphs to a Brief Life*. His story, through my recollection and imagination, is small, incomplete, fragmented (what the novelist Juvenal Acosta calls "Vidas menores"). And if it is only minor, I can write only modest moments. We stand around a kitchen table in silence, peer into a box of food, and I have to accept that I don't have the words to describe my father's longing, his path from his island home to this kitchen. The more I delve into my memories of my father, the more I realize his life is an unfinished book; it continues to grow the more I try to write it, new pages revealing themselves day after day, as if this growing will go on without end. Even if I take the next twenty years to write it, I won't make his life and story any more complete. The story will still be fragmented, small, minor, adrift in a turbulent sea between a kitchen and an island, between a father and a son.

⁎⁎

The kitchen was the warmest room in the apartment. On the table my father's box of food was filled with fire—the orange juice we drank, the food we ate, a moment that had to be burned from memory because who would ever want to remember it, who would ever want to talk about it. Off the kitchen was my bedroom, the only room without heat. Half an hour or so before bedtime, my mother would turn on the electric heater placed a few feet from my bed. When I opened the door, I stepped through and quickly closed it and ran across the room and slid under the blanket. It was like lying on a frozen lake, the blanket and sheets cold as wet snow falling across my face and neck when I lay on the ground, arms flying up and down, trying to make a snow angel. I watched my breath rise and fill with the muted moonlight falling through the window, swirl, and disappear into the dark. I scratched a hole through the icy window, and the backyard instantly filled with the white light, the tall oak tree turning blue. Once my legs warmed I turned on my bedside lamp, put the thick *Little House in the Big Woods* on my lap, and began to read. The thin pages sounded so crisp, complete, and whole against the continuous drone of the electric heater, the coils a million miniscule flames. The young Laura Wilder looked out her frozen window too. At night she sometimes felt hunger and longed to escape in her imagination, and remembered that even the most unremarkable of Pa's labors were there as she looked into the big dark woods.

It seems unfair to remember my childhood as happy. My father may have been desperate in ways I didn't understand, and I hadn't yet learned at school that I should be ashamed of being poor and working class. If someone asked, *Did you have a happy childhood?* I would say, *No.* But my parents weren't at fault. How can I blame them for being young and poor?

My father's aqua blue truck was like the sea, blue in green, and even now as I let the color flash in memory I'm bathed in warm waters. My father was trying to make something happen—every day, out in the cold snow, he was picking up trash and searching out new customers. He was working hard. That's what I'd say. I'd tell them: His eyes and jaw were like steel most of the time, and I tried not to look at them too closely when he drove around. I tried not to notice too much the bottle of whiskey he pulled from under the seat and took long drinks from. He turned up the music, smiled, and laughed when he hit a patch of ice and his truck swerved, causing me to laugh too when my stomach dropped. I loved the way his shoulders shifted, his hands moving on the wheel. And when he slowed down behind a loading dock to let me get out, I ran as fast as I could to grab a box by a dumpster, and as I ran back to his truck I felt that in my own small way I was helping him work. And, even if for only a moment, there was something there I should call happy, something I never wanted to end, because it burned in the palms of my hands.

Puerto Rican House

I was striking my fist into my baseball glove. In between the whacks, my palm warming, I felt the air around me change. Across the street, a man lifted his left leg over a strand of wire, ducked underneath, and stepped through. Standing in the driveway alongside the house, he looked down at his right hand and flipped a dark-handled knife—the blade shiny gray-blue—into the tall grass. His forehead was streaked with sweat, his curly hair wet as if he'd been walking in the rain. For the briefest of moments he caught me there, stared at me, his eyes deep and red, as if he wanted to remember me forever. He wiped his hands on his thighs. He ran away.

I had been throwing a rubber ball against the front steps of our house. There were three cement steps, and depending on which step I threw at, the rubber ball would return as a high fly, a line drive, or a grounder. I hit the top one a bit too high and hard and the ball flew above my head, just out of reach, out into the street. A car slammed on its brakes in a long screech, the white-and-gray-cracked ball bouncing on the hood to the windshield, slowly rolling down to the street before resting against the curb. I heard the voices from across the street rise in a mock cheer. I stepped across the sidewalk and reached down for my ball.

On the open concrete porch the men were like shadows sitting on chairs and crates, leaning against the black aluminum porch posts or back against the front of the house, their hands folded behind them. Dressed in T-shirts or white, light blue, or yellow guayaberas. I couldn't make out their eyes underneath their hat brims. I felt deep within—as my shoulders scrunched together and collapsed, and my head dropped—that they watched and said things about my every move. A barrage of words in a raspy voice crossed the street, something sharp in the tone, followed by a chorus of laughter. From a wrinkled bag the brown neck of a whiskey bottle glinted in the sun. The front screen door opened, a dark figure looking out toward the street, and Juan stood up from his milk crate and went inside.

It was Juan's apartment. He wasn't very tall, he had thin black hair combed back over his ears, long and greasy in the back, and he always wore a brown felt fedora, a sleeveless undershirt, slacks, and cheap sandals. He had a mustache, and his dark eyes were wrinkled around the edges. He sat in a stuffed brown cloth chair, his belly small and rounded, staring, thinking, and taking long swallows from a bottle. He was a magnet that drew other Puerto Rican men— his friends who had arrived in the 1960s to work at the Green Giant mushroom cannery, and, over time, others passing by who walked up the steps to join them. My father would take me to Juan's, and winter afternoons we'd sit in his bare living room, the air hot and dusty and the light as yellowed as Juan's undershirt. The bottoms of his brown pants were rolled up a few times, and the skin on his ankles and feet was dry and chalky white; deep cracks ran along his heals, and his toenails were long and sharp. There was a sour milky smell I couldn't locate, could only shiver if I thought about it too much, and found it best to breathe through my mouth. He sat in his chair like a Buddha, and he and my father began to talk. My father was drying out, trying to find a job, and Juan understood. They sat quietly, breathing evenly as cars passed in the slushy street and the wind rattled the windows. The yellow light slowly drained from the room, dusk rising outside the windows, and I sat as still as possible and felt (what I later learned to name) winter's lonely consolation.

One day I was lying on my stomach up in my room, skipping around in my Civil War encyclopedia. The drummer boy played, I heard the boom of cannon fire and screaming men, saw smoke drifting across the battlefield. The front door clicked open and then slammed shut. My father had been gone all day across the street. Their voices rose in the kitchen, something crashed like a broken window, and their voices rose higher. I rolled over on my back, looked up through the top of my bedroom window, the sky a deep blue, the tree bare and gold, a single dead brown leaf caught in a handlike branch shaking in the wind. I will never forget my mother's words: *What do you do over there? What's so special? You'd think you're all a bunch of queers.*

My father stood on our front porch holding his machete. He squinted, the skin around his left eye was scraped and bloody, and the skin at his hairline looked as if strips had been torn from his face. He was shirtless, and his machete trembled in his hand as he stared across the street. My mother's voice was urgent: *You have to put the machete away. Are you crazy?*

I stepped away from the porch, tucked my glove and ball under my arm. Then I heard the roar of an engine, turned back to the street, and caught the blur of blue as the state police cruiser sped by and halted in front of the Puerto Rican House. I felt or heard something stronger than the spinning lights and wailing sirens. He ducked. Stopped. Looked at me. He threw the knife in the grass and ran away.

He had arrived in June after being released from Jackson Prison. He wore fancy long-sleeved shirts of silk profusely emblazoned with flowers or circles or fruits, the top three buttons undone, a long gold chain with a cross lying over his hairy chest. He had a thick, long mustache, curly dark brown hair, and mocha skin. His eyes were red and watery—he was loud, boisterous, and always drunk. I'd hide behind a tree and watch. He paced the porch, his voice filled with anger or cutting jest, his arms wildly gesturing, and the veins on the back of his hands like ropes when he pointed at someone's chest or face. An electric mystery outlined his body. Where had he come from before prison? What did he ever do to end up in Jackson? And what—out of all the places in the world—what brought him to the Puerto Rican House? What was his name?

He didn't run very far. He was now handcuffed, a state trooper on each side holding an arm as they walked him down the middle of the street. His brown shirt with falling pineapples still looked pressed and clean, his gold cross bouncing on his chest, but anyone could see that his lower buttons were also open, and if you looked closely the silk had been torn and the buttons were gone. Small lines of blood ran from his hair and mixed with the sweat on his forehead. A trooper opened the cruiser's back door, a hand pushed the top of his head, and he was stuffed into the backseat.

An ambulance—sirens blazing—came down the street. The EMTs ran up the stairs and crossed the porch and went inside. My father stood in the street with a shirt on now, his machete put away. My mother called for me to go inside. I stepped onto the street. She called me again. When the EMTs came out of Juan's apartment,

Raphael walked between them. Bone-thin Raphi, dark chocolate skin, black hair swept off his head elegantly with pomade, his face—usually smooth, smiling, beautiful—hard as stone. He was shirtless and his ribs were wrapped with wide bands of gauze and tape, the gauze very white against his skin. I walked closer, and when he looked at me his eyes seemed vacant, as if he no longer recognized me. Raphi grabbed the steel handle on the back of the ambulance to step inside, his biceps muscle tightening, shaking, and then slack as his body crumpled into itself—*whoa, take it easy, hold on there*—and the EMTs gathered behind him, held him steady, and guided him into the ambulance.

Earlier, when I stood at the edge of the porch, I had watched the knife float in the air, weightless, the thick brown handle's brass pin sparking in the sun, transforming into blue steel and shadow as it fell and disappeared in the grass. My left hand had tingled, my middle finger burning, and I palmed the ball within my glove harder. It had scared me to see my father that way, caught there in a moment of indecision on the front porch, as he tucked his machete behind his back inside his belt. The cuts and scrapes on the side of his eye looked so raw, wet, and tender. His profile blurred, swirled, and then sharpened into clarity as if I was looking at a developing photograph: the outlines of two staring faces merged into a single face of scared anger. It was then that I could see myself walking across the street with a machete or a knife, knowing that more than defending myself I needed to hurt, perhaps even kill, another man.

*
**

The royal blue cruiser, the blue-and-gray uniforms of the state troopers, the blue tree shadows, and the sky mirrored in the back window of the cruiser clouding out the man inside as he was driven away. The blue steel of the knife falling into the grass. The bruise next to my father's eye: the man had shoved my father off the porch and into the thorny bush, his face and eye scraped and cut as he fell through and hit the ground.

⁎

The roll of black electrical tape bounced on the table, rolled across the top, fell to the floor. When I had tried to catch the end of the tape, the knife jumped off the edge, sliced across my knuckle, down into the web of skin between my index and middle fingers. A thick pool of blood quickly rose between them. Drops hitting the floor— red, maroon—as I hurried to the bathroom and tried to stop the bleeding. I had to stop it. I didn't want my father to see what I had done, and when I looked down at my hand, lifting the soaked piece of toilet paper, the blood rose faster than before, and the cut seemed to catch on fire. I closed my eyes: I saw my father's face hard with rage for a hospital bill he couldn't afford. I looked for a place to hide the knife.

⁎

The four black-and-white furry ankles tied with blue string to the rusty fire escape. The ankles of the rabbits I feed every morning before leaving for school. My father must have first broken their necks with his hands, tied their back legs to the fire escape to skin them, and then cut their pink-and-blue bodies off just above their ankles to cook a stew. *Conejo. Conejo estofado. Smothered rabbit.* He and his friends will eat well tonight. I look closely at the string around their ankles, tied just like I tie my shoes, even if the tips of their furry feet, stained with blood, do not look like shoes. I cry and cry and cry into the night, my face hot, tears streaming.

The sound of his yelling. He was in the kitchen and I don't know how he gathered the strength: my father, barefoot, kicked the table into the air and onto its side, a bowl of rice shattering, the clatter of silverware, and the table thudding against the floor. He limped around the kitchen in a jerking circle trying not to put any weight on his foot. The back door slammed shut. His big toe swollen, the nail a bubble of blue blood. In the bathroom, my father crouched in the tub, naked, hot water falling on his foot. Through the steam I handed him his knife. He sliced into his nail, grunted, and released the blood that slowly swirled down the drain.

Growing up across the street from the Puerto Rican House I stored away blue memories. Those men—standing or sitting in a bluish-gray light—were the sentries who watched my every move, a chorus that commented on all they witnessed—our house, my family, my father, my childhood. For the longest time I tried to ignore them—erase them from memory—and yet, as I grow toward their age, they have slowly taken residency within my life, they flow in my blood, and when I look in the mirror I still see them standing in the shadows, close enough to touch my shoulder, cup my elbow. I might have walked through one door, down a hallway or alleyway, driven down a different road, gone to work at some factory or in some field, and ended up hanging out at a bar on the edge of town or standing on the front porch of a gray house. I might have been the one who was stabbed or who had stabbed. I might have easily died and been forgotten along the way. Like many of those Puerto Rican men of my father's generation, I could've simply become the dust in a region of lost names.

*
**

I take up the knife and slowly clean it in scalding water, fingers and nails rubbing and scraping along the blade. I place an onion on the cutting board, some *ají dulce* peppers, a potato, and a few carrots. I chop them up. I smash the knife flat against garlic. I sauté it all with olive oil in a big pan. I add salt, pepper, cumin, paprika, and a bouquet of cilantro, oregano, and culantro. The knife cuts the rabbit as if it was butter, and I drop the pieces into the pan and brown them. I add a can of tomato sauce and two cups of water. My father and his friends sit around the table talking and laughing. Someone's telling a story of how as a child he stacked cut cane across his back and carried it, crouching low to the ground, to a cart in the red dirt lane. How there was nothing better than cold water to rinse away the sweat and the smoke from the burning fields. How sweet to have clear eyes. Juan raises his glass of rum in a toast. My father takes a long drink, his head tipped back, eyes closed. Raphi smiles. They seem happy, filled with something I might call pride or forgiveness or memory. There's an empty chair. They wait for me to join them.

Almost Blue

My father didn't punch my mother's face as much as shove it, the heel of his hand under her jaw, her head snapping back against the bedroom door. Her shoulder banged against the doorjamb, her arms reaching out as if to block my father's hand or to grab hold of something before she fell.

My father was always filled with a rage I couldn't understand. Where did it come from? What caused it? All I felt were the results: my father's hard *cocotasos* (his knuckles like steel rapping on the top of my skull), him striking my forehead with a thrown board, or the end of his hammer's handle on my shoulder or elbow, his sudden screaming, so loud and close I could smell the sweet rum on his breath. Once, a friend and I were alone in the house. We were very young, maybe four or five, and we took turns drinking from a carton of milk, holding the milk in our mouths, and then slowly spitting it into each other's face. When my father came home he took down the leather strap he hung from a nail on the wood post in the middle of the kitchen. He whipped me and whipped me until I almost passed out. My shoulders burned as if the thin leather sliced deeper into my skin at every lash. Another time, a friend and I had a pillow fight. I hit him so hard in the face that he lost his balance, fell back against the couch, and slid to the floor. He stormed out of the house, kicking the bottom of the new aluminum screen door my father had just put up, leaving it broken and crinkled like cheap tin foil. That night I couldn't throw a strike to save my life. Nausea and fear churned in my stomach, rose into my shoulders and arms as I stood on the mound. Each inning was an eternity, and my pitching became more and more erratic. My father sat in the crowd on the top of a picnic table looking down on the field, his face dark in the shadows and his shoulders like concrete. One walk after another. Pitches into the dirt, over the batter's head, striking against the chain-link backstop. Between innings my friend sat at the other end of the dugout, arms crossed, his face beet red, his jaw hard. I wished I could stay in the dugout for the whole night.

I blamed or excused my father's anger on his drinking. His yelling and belittling and hitting were actions he couldn't control. When he was drunk he didn't know what he was doing, and he probably didn't remember afterward. His hangovers were painful and timeless, and how could he be blamed when he was so miserable? There were the shaking hands and arms, the slow tremors in his shoulders, his nervousness when he tried to stop drinking. His body in the throes of a nightmare. He had every right, I suppose, to be angry, to hate the world, his life, maybe even me: a mouth to feed, a body to clothe, a living memory of his lost childhood. I couldn't talk about school, a game, or fishing—they were not of any interest to him; they must've seemed frivolous in comparison to his working life. He didn't have the words to express feelings like that. He didn't have a language—in Spanish or English—for my childhood. Moments would build, time slowly passing as his frustration and anger grew. Then I'd feel his knuckles on my skull for doing something or nothing. I was *estúpido* for talking, for spilling some milk, for not being fast enough or strong enough when he needed help to change a carburetor, fix a door, or weed his garden. Sometimes a few months of sobriety passed and he was still angry. He couldn't discover his own island of peace in this shipwreck called Michigan, and without it he couldn't let the waters of forgiveness raise his craft, and so how could he ever forgive the world or himself? The energy of his drinking was on the frantic edge of beautiful—a lovely, poetic frenzy. How he picked up a long birthday cake with yellow flowers and green vines from the table, carried it quickly and perfectly balanced on his flat palm, and then smashed it in the trashcan without a single frosted flower falling to the floor. His livid, loud, solitary conversations in a darkened room, Spanish flying like a bat in the twilight from one corner to the other, various emotions and tones becoming other screaming selves dancing across the ceiling, my father swinging and sweating in some demonic battle to save his life. And then the immense silence when he stopped, followed by the rush of his urine striking the wall and floor as he pissed in some hallucinated bathroom. His joyous laughter rising and thinning into one long note, like a lone trumpet blowing from an open window, a tattered red curtain swaying from within. Upstairs, downstairs, room to room following the blaring music from his stereo, my violin up against his bare chest and chin as he tried to capture the notes he alone heard, his hand raking the bow across the strings. Sitting on the edge of the bed, the violin across his lap, with one eye closed, he minutely inspected the instrument, tried to figure out how to remove the bridge so it might become a guitar. The circular path he walked in the living room, a strobe light playing along the wall, the carpet darkening into a path as if he were walking through wet grass.

Peering around the corner of the doorway, I found him sitting on the couch. I became transfixed by how quickly he could pack, unpack, and repack his suitcase, his hand finally clutching the handle, raising the suitcase for a moment to assay its weight. The satisfaction on his face was immediate: he was now ready to go who knows where. In less than four minutes he was ready to hit the road.

We are both shirtless. The camera very close, our chests and faces big and clear, the background blurred like smoke. Flash. Our skin golden, still tan from summer Connecticut beaches. I'm very young, my hair still sandy blond and vivid next to my father's black duck-tail and sideburns. Flash. We are both smiling. My father and I have been arm wrestling in one of the photos. In the other, we have our arms around each other's shoulders, chests softly touching because we've been hugging. These are the faded snapshots I still try to carry in memory. Flash. On the other side of my father's rage: *un abrazo fuerte.*

Back in the living room my father was sitting next to me on the couch, his suitcase between us. He was wearing his winter coat and a funny-looking pillbox cap, Russian-like, the edges above his ears a soft black fur that curled and shined. He punched me in the thigh. He had lost his job. He was sitting so close, yelling, *You see what happens when you don' do what'I say?* He punched me again. *Don't blame him,* my mother said as she entered the room. *This is your fault.* He stood up. *It's your own fault, no one else's. Ay, shut up–you don' know.* They yelled, cursed. He picked up his suitcase. Looked down at me. *See what happens. I have to go.* My mother said something, he yelled, swung his suitcase, threw it, rushed forward.

I remember her black turtleneck, her jeans, her tan boots with red laces, her right leg coming up to kick him square between the legs, how he lost his breath, his eyes emptied, and he crumpled, his hands between his legs, to his knees. I laughed, silently, and let out the long breath that he was still holding. Cold tears running down my face.

That night he was gone. Gone away back to Connecticut and his family. And then even farther: if he could work it out, he'd fly back to Puerto Rico.

Later, in the summer, he was back. No work. Had been drunk for months. My mother's father was in the VA hospital outside Chicago for bypass surgery. She wanted to be there but was afraid to leave home. One evening I'm watching a Cubs and Phillies game. My father's pacing like an animal in a cage, prowling between drinks, filled with unlimited energy and anger. He goes outside, takes a drink from a bottle in a paper sack under the back steps, comes back in and settles down for a time at the kitchen table. Then he finds me lying on the couch. He turns off the game. He's decided that he wants to paint the fence. He tells me to get my shoes. Twilight purples the living room window. I say *it's too late, why not tomorrow. Get your shoes.* I run upstairs, hear his yelling, a broken glass or plate, a slammed door.

When my mother finds me I am crying, my face buried in my pillow. She asks in a raspy voice what happened. When I turn around, I see her pale face, and as her hands try to pull her housecoat up around her neck, my stomach tumbles and I feel how weak she is. In a whisper she tells me to come back downstairs, my father's gone. I can finish watching the game. She goes back to bed.

I'm there on the couch again, my father next to me, and he says, *See what happens when you don' do what'I say.* He had been gone all night, his bloodshot eyes are sharp knives, his right hand clenched into a fist against his knee. He punches me. My mother steps from the bedroom. She can barely speak. *Leave him alone.* Veins rise along her neck but her voice sounds miles away. She looks paler, her hands white and cold. She had become ill, needed a tonsillectomy, and only a few days out of the hospital she's still sick, filled with regret, still grieving because she could not visit her father before he died. My father starts yelling. She tries to yell back. *Stop. Please stop, can't you see? I was just in the hospital . . . I can't take it.* They are standing close. *You shut up,* and his hand rises, *you stupid hillbilly,* his fist closing. My scalp grows hot. Legs shaking. I'm trying to stand. To get up and throw myself between them . . .

And there is my father's hand rising to her face, and just before he punches her, his hand opens just a little so the heel of his hand pushes her jaw, her head snapping back.

For some reason, I don't know why, my mother's brother is standing in the living room, and he's yelling at my father to *stop, stop, what are you doing.* My father steps away, rears back his arm, and punches the bedroom door, his knuckles breaking through. He turns to my uncle, ready to scream, swings and misses, stumbles, and my uncle doesn't have to push very hard for my father to fall to the floor.

Memories don't arrive chronologically or voluntarily—they bloom one after the other like flowers in the spring, colorful and full one day from dirt that still smells of winter, like spots of blood appearing on a tile floor when you don't even know you've been cut. I never have to search for them or call them forth. Sometimes it's the smell of coffee. Sometimes it's the sound of a hummingbird approaching the screened-in porch. Sometimes it's my fist closed around the handle of a knife. Sometimes it's the heat of the sun on my scalp, and though I'm standing on a beach looking at waves crashing white against the sand, what I picture inside myself is a darkened room, me and my father sitting on a couch or standing in the middle of the room, and we are not alone because his rage—like an arched wave—stands between us. The dark blue veins on his hand like hard, knotted muscles, like strong, swift streams, and in his face I see where the streams begin: his clenched jaw and his heart throbbing in his temples.

We've never had any reason to talk about the past. There are days when I tell myself: *There is no memory. None of this ever happened. These are only your intimate intervals.* Yet somewhere in Ohio on his way to Connecticut my father's car ran off the road and became mired in a field. There were weekends when he wasn't home because he was serving time in jail for too many drunk-driving arrests. There were days when he lived a different life in Chicago. There were the years when he had no driver's license. And I can never forget how scared I was when it seemed so true that my mother was dying. How pale she was for it being summer. How I was the one in the car with her as she pulled over, opened her door, and lifted a paper towel printed with faint tulips, almost blue, and pressed it to her lips and spit out the thick blood clotting in her throat.

For days after, my mother in the hospital again, and I thought of nothing else: Mom almost died, my mother will die. A fist breaks wood can break a face. You can choke on your own blood.

My father gone again. Days melted into weeks, pooled into months, my stomach flooded in torrents of fear and pain. There I sit on the edge of my bed looking through the window into the bare tree, the thin wet branches pointing fingers: *There are no questions to ask, no one to turn to, you hold your throat. Yes, you, yes, this is all your fault.* I clench my fists, cross my arms and hold them under my armpits. I rock back and forth, begin to hum. I raise my right fist and begin pounding my thigh, thud after thud. My knuckles strike beyond skin and flesh to meet bone. Pain turns to heat until a perfect circle of numbness rises. My fist turns to my stomach, punch after punch, just on the edge of my ribs. My midsection warms. The room stills in the day's last light. I listen to my fist. My stomach as hard and smooth as the window glazed with rain and shadows. I listen for something—anything—that sounds like forgetting.

Always True

He was rinsing off the cut-up rabbit, some of the pieces pink with lines of white, the legs and thighs looking blue, almost as if the meat had been bruised. At the bottom of the sink glistening with blood and water lay his long wood-handled knife. He shook each piece over the sink and returned it to the plate. He had a bowl filled with flour and he sprinkled it with salt, black pepper, garlic powder, oregano, and mixed it with his fingertips. He rolled the pieces of rabbit in the flour, first dipping each in a shallow bowl of milk, and then laid them in the cast iron skillet of hot oil that was beginning to smoke. Each piece made the oil bubble more quickly and filled the kitchen with the sound of rushing water. He didn't have any lights on. The kitchen stood in a cube of gray light that fell from the window over the sink. The flames underneath the skillet glowed like a lamp. He was shirtless and barefoot in black slacks. Instead of making a red wine vinegar *soncocho* or a tomato-based *estofado*, he fried the rabbit. The pieces were brown and crispy when he lifted them from the skillet with a fork and placed them on a plate covered with paper towels, the blue print bleeding with grease.

I had stepped into the kitchen after spending the day down along the river, the fish not biting, and lying for the longest time in the cool grass shaded by a circle of river birches thinking about my mother in the hospital. The sun fell through the deep green leaves that turned silver when their undersides flashed in the breeze, gray clouds passed and the grass became cooler, and I thought as long as it doesn't rain, as long as I don't get soaked, then today won't be the day my mother dies.

My father didn't turn around, didn't seem to know or care that I was there. He had not cooked for anyone but himself. He bent over the plate, lifted a piece of rabbit, and ate greedily as I listened to him chew and suck and blow air through his mouth to cool the hot meat before swallowing. The batter crunched, his lips smacked together, and small sounds of pleasure rose from his chest as if he were humming, followed by his hard swallows. Then just as soon as it all began it stopped. The piece of rabbit fell to the counter. He moved directly over the sink, his head leaning forward, his hands clenching the edges. He tried to cough, gagged, struck his chest several times, and coughed again. His black hair suddenly became electric in the silver light as he bent his head over the sink, tried to cough, and pulled back chocking. He turned around, his eyes dark, still pools, and struck his chest again. His mouth wide open. He couldn't scream a word. He looked straight into my eyes, waiting for me to say something. I grabbed his right arm, pushed his left shoulder, and turned him back toward the sink. Instinctively one hand became a fist, the other clasped around it, and they found their way to the middle of his stomach, a bit high and just under his ribs. I pulled my fist as hard as I could and lifted. He gagged. I pulled again. Felt my knuckles against his ribs, and in one quick and hard jerk his breath returned with a long exhale, and a bone clinked in the bottom of the sink against his knife.

When my father turned around his hands were trembling, he let out a long, terrible wail, his shoulders shaking and his ribs heaving. Tears streamed down his cheeks. His face twisted in grief. He picked up the plate of fried rabbit and dumped it into the trash. He cried, deep, jagged breaths, and slammed the plate into the trashcan.

I have no recollection of how I ended up in my mother and father's bedroom that evening. I only remember being in the dark room, his arm tightly around me, his hot body, and his fits of screaming and crying. A humid summer night. No fan. The shades drawn. And the sweat from his chest warm and sticky on my back. He shuddered and screamed, called out for my mother, yelled *no no no no* . . . each time holding me tighter. I couldn't sleep, the heat too much, suffocating, and each time I was on the verge of sleep my father would shudder—my eyes quickly opening—as if in his sleep he dreamed he were falling from the top of a building or holding on tightly as the plane that carried him fell toward the sea. A weak breeze pushed out the bottom of the shade, a brief crack that let me see across the dark street and catch a glimpse of a single light bulb hanging in the Puerto Rican House.

There was no one I could turn to, no way to escape his strong hands, and I tried to imagine that my father's nightmares were his prayers for forgiveness for hitting my mother and sending her back to the hospital. I was unimportant that night, but I was his son and at least I could help him get through his fear and pain. The smell of whiskey leaking from his body anointed me with some dark harmony of resolve, and as I stared at the shade, the edge of the sill, waiting for first light, I hoped maybe to hear some talk and laughter from across the street, and then someone yelling for my father to come over for a drink, a game of dice, or just to talk. Only silence. The creak of the shade. My father's soft breathing as he finally quieted and slept.

When a thin strip of dawn appeared, I slipped from his hands and arms and stood facing the door. Unsure of where to go or what to do, I started to shake with fright that one night could become so sad. In the mirror the reflected shade trembled and the crack of light let in bright rays that bounced off and fell on top of the bureau, a black comb, some loose change in a silver dish.

Years passed, yet no matter how far I thought I had traveled from my father, I was still in his room on that hot summer night, and I saw that no matter how long I stayed with him, there were many details I'd never know. For how could I ever know his pain, how could I ever know a night of such vulnerability? How, in the end, could I ever know my father's love? And so how could I ever understand his love for my mother?

I am sitting at my Amish table, a steaming cup of black coffee next to my hand, a birch and cedar fire in the brick hearth warming my legs and hands. It is May 8 and it snowed yesterday and again this morning. Last week it had been close to 80°, and outside the window I have a new garden to look at. The neighbors ripped out some scraggly old bushes, landscaped a small hill of soil and cedar chips in the corner closest to my window, and planted five fir trees in a row ascending from about two feet all the way up to five. They planted a few holly bushes too. In the very corner is a giant, jagged rock streaked with green moss, Zen-like, solid, maybe forever, thinly covered with snow. I have never met the neighbors, have seen them only in passing. Nevertheless I feel as if they built it all for me, so when I sit at my table, alone in this room, looking out the window, that landscaped corner garden is mine. It reflects a favorite passage from Henry Miller:

> I find there is plenty of room in the world for everybody—great inter-
> spatial depths, great ego universes, great islands of repair, for who-
> ever attains individuality. On the surface, where the historical battles

rage, where everything is interpreted in terms of money and power, there may be crowding, but life only begins when one drops below the surface, when one gives up the struggle, sinks and disappears from sight. Now I can easily not write as write: there is no longer any compulsion, no longer any therapeutic aspect to it. Whatever I do is done out of sheer joy: I drop my fruits like a ripe tree. (*The Wisdom of the Heart*)

My father, I realize, looking toward my garden, was never a horrible person—I should've never accepted that others see him as terrible, a failure, a man not worthy of story let alone remembrance. He drank with a passion because it was his eloquent expression, even if it was in a language no one wanted to listen to. In that room, on that hot and humid summer night when we were both so afraid that my mother was dying, he may have felt that his life began below the surface, and as he drank and dreamed, gave up the struggle and sank, he disappeared into his own song. There, on a dark blue night, he offered me his *canción* as he held me and cried on his own island of repair.

Once the garden was done, the neighbors installed a knee-high wrought-iron fence between the garden and the sidewalk. As if that could stop me this morning from claiming it. I can put down my pen, get up from my table, step outside, and cross the yard to sit down on my dark and mossy rock.

Blue in Green

A turquoise pickup stops at the light. A man grips the steering wheel, his knuckles like black walnuts, the tops smudged with oil. He turns. A thick mustache covers his mouth, his hair–black and unruly–is parted down the middle and swept back by hand, grease and dirt streaking his forehead. The oil on his knuckles snakes along his wrists and up his arms, his jacket sleeves pushed to his elbows. His arms are raised level with the steering wheel, his shoulders wide, the jacket collar pulled up around his ears. The truck begins to roll through the intersection. There's no tailgate, and the heavy load bunches together: an engine block sprouting hoses and red and yellow wires; a doorless refrigerator, its insides cracked and stained; sheets of dented and crinkled aluminum siding; twisted lengths of steel pipe and copper tubing. This unknown man slowly driving away, and across his back, like letters spread across a neon sign, is your last name emblazoned in gold on the dark blue fabric.

The truck slows on the Main Street rise–a rattle of metal, white smoke chugging from the tailpipe–and then descends toward the river and the setting sun. The Ready Theatre's red-bordered white marquee, a perfect rectangle like the front of an envelope, its black letters–Two for One Admission Tonight– floating within a square of clear bulbs that tint the air soft topaz. The man's not wearing any old jacket. It's a Niles High School jacket. He's wearing the jacket that you once wore, the jacket that bears your name. The air grows colder, heavier along your arms, and charges the night beginning to rise on the street corner. You stand perfectly still, stare toward the orange-streaked horizon. You have to make sure that what you glimpsed is true.

**

I had saved up some money—from a paper route, shoveling snow, selling salmon, working in the fields—or maybe I had pestered my mother about how I desperately needed a school jacket. In high school jocks wore navy blue jackets with collars striped in blue and gold, our school colors, the same pattern of stripes banded around the cuffs, and on the back the boy's last name. Sometimes an earned junior varsity letter—a huge gold *N*—was stitched to the front left side. At the beginning of the seventh grade I wanted a school jacket more than anything. One evening after my mother got home from work, she took me down to the sporting goods store. The salesman laid the jacket across the counter, the sleeves spread wide, my name in large gold block letters. Bright. Crisp. Threads stitched around each letter smooth and strong. He lifted the jacket, looked at me without a word, and as I turned he slipped it over my arms and shoulders. A perfect fit across the chest, a little loose on my stomach so I could thrust my hands deep into the pockets when walking in the cold. The snap buttons clicked together like dice hitting a brick wall.

You would've probably needed a new jacket soon anyway, my mother said. *It's money well spent.* The inside of her yellow Bug glowed with the jacket's white and gold and blue stripes.

She had ordered a jacket that was different from everyone else's. The dark blue polyester was of a slicker and shinier material, and instead of just blue and gold stripes banding the fabric on the wrists and collar, my jacket had white lines between the blue and gold, which actually made the colors stand out, made them cleaner and distinct. Being that it was cheaper, it made the jacket all the more affordable. After my initial excitement for the jacket I was disappointed by the differences. Why couldn't I have the same jacket as everyone else? Why did my jacket have to stand out? After walking around town a few times, wearing it to school, seeing it in my room hanging on the back of the door, I grew to love the jacket, loved its newness, the bright and clean colors, my name in big letters across the back. There seemed something special in walking around town in that jacket. It held some mystery that made me feel like a kid who belonged.

At the time, my father was living in Chicago. A few months after I got the jacket he returned, and it didn't take very long for him to once again begin drinking. Drunk for weeks at a time, sometimes gone for days, it was as if his hands and lips burned for a bottle, and then I would walk into the house some late afternoon and find him passed out on the couch, an arm draped over his eyes. He liked my jacket. At first it was comical, even fun, to watch him stumble around the living room with my jacket on, the sleeves pushed to his elbows, the collar flipped up, barefoot in black slacks, his hair combed back with pomade, an eight track of the Beatles, Three Dog Night, Chicago, or some *plena* I've forgotten playing loudly in the background, his small black strobe light flashing against the walls and carpet. When he danced around, I could see the jacket's buttons had been snapped together about halfway up, leaving his chest hair visible. He said something about liking the colors, the stripes, it was almost his size. He undid a few buttons and then snapped them up quickly, his ears waiting for that metallic sound. He never asked if he could wear it. If he had, I could've never said no. The jacket fit him well, and it was his last name too.

One morning in a rush for school I slipped the jacket on and ran for the front door only to stop short as I met the harsh smell of cigarettes and whiskey, as if my father's invisible body, out in the night, was still inside my jacket.

When I return to that half-lit room, the strobe light flashing scattered circles of silver and black along the walls and the carpet, I hear the sound of my father's arms moving to the music as the jacket's sleeves rub against his sides, see for a moment my last name cloaked in shadows, and stand there within the lie of my life: although I did not hesitate to have it placed on the back of a jacket, I was ashamed of my name. No one knew how to pronounce it, and I never liked to pronounce it. *How do you say your name? What kind of name is that? Where are you from?* A knife stabbed into my stomach: I flinched and silence filled me.

Having my name sewed onto a jacket did not change it; it was still strange and unpronounceable and foreign. I didn't understand that many would see the name on the back of the jacket as silly, meaningless, a joke. I was too naïve to realize that the jacket wouldn't all of a sudden make me popular, part of the crowd—it wouldn't help me to create, or even imagine, a new life. I was still a boy from somewhere else.

My father never had any reason to talk of his name. As silent as he was, never sharing that much in Spanish, hardly ever a word in English, his language found in work, drink, his fevered days of drunkenness, why would he talk about a name? A man of little words, his name became the smallest of words until it receded into a place where it could no longer be heard, let alone spoken, a cenotaph to regions of memory I'll never know.

I knew it was Spanish, but after growing up bilingual in Connecticut, I, like my father, was shipwrecked in Michigan, where our name didn't have a place in English. I never cared for learning and was often in trouble at school for being disruptive. I was not a writer who obsessed over every image, sentence, and scene as I worked in the early morning light with words. What did I know of Rilke's "pure mornings"? Growing up I never called him father, dad, papa, or papi. Never pops. I always called him Chago, a name as lost to me as Arroyo. From my first words he was Chago. Sometimes, when I called him, I thought I saw his chin slightly drop, the tip of his hat cover his eyes. He would bend into the weeds, swing and slice with his machete, or bend into his plants and pick some beans and drop them with a ping into a pail. What did I know of names?

Much later I came across the name Iago, and I wondered if there was some connection to Chago. Each time I said them together, there, between their immediate lovely sounds, there were images, memories, and words I wanted to name. In their sound and echo I started to imagine an uncut page in a long-lost book, and once the page was cut I read a single name, Santiago, which held inside of it Iago, and by that logic it also held Chago. Suddenly the names were free—they had sounds in Puerto Rico, sounds in America, sounds in England, sounds in Spain, and as they traveled from country to country, from here to there, from there to here, they were embarking on a new journey. I could now say my father's full name: *Santiago Arroyo Perez*. If I were ever to understand the mystery of my father's life, I had to listen closely to names as they moved from language to language, from country to country. I had to listen closely to names in order to find my father. As I listened to Chago, the only name I had ever called him, *Chago* finally spoke to me with greater urgency, and I heard the ultimate link: Chago is the diminutive of Santiago, like Jim to James, like Jack to James. Chago is the junior of

Santiago. My father is his father's son by blood and name. Between my father and his father they shared Santiago.

When I was born my parents gave me an old-fashioned, awkward name. Only a first name and a last name. Whenever I write my name, I must always leave the space between the two names blank. My parents couldn't imagine a middle name that sounded good between my first and last. It seems my parents thus fated me to listen closely to names, and as well to never ignore a silence, to never forget that sometimes the power of words is found in the silences.

In that long-ago living room the strobe light still throws circles against the wall and carpet. Outside the dusk grows, inside the shadows deepen, my father caught there for a moment within the pulse of music and light, day and night, my father dancing with his eyes closed. I have to see him there wearing my jacket, his arms swaying at his sides, and without either of us uttering a word, I hear that by being in that room together, as father and son, we are beginning to say—even in our separate silences, we are beginning to write—*Arroyo*.

One night my father went out, and when he returned the next morning he was no longer wearing my jacket. I easily picture a dark living room. There is one brown upholstered chair, a few folding chairs creating a half-circle in front of it. Beer cans litter the floor, and on a table covered with a pockmarked plastic cloth a few bottles of Canadian Club and some smudged glasses. A naked bulb hangs over the table, the bottles glinting in its light. I hear a voice. There, by the front door, he's talking to a new man in town, hand on his shoulder, his words coming out fast. No, my father says; no, he doesn't know

of any work, he'll ask around. He tells a man with dark, bushy hair
it's cold outside. My father closes the front door. He tells the man
over and over again he must take his jacket, it's too cold—this is no
longer Puerto Rico—to walk in the snow without one. Somebody
bumps the bulb, and light and shadow sway along the wall. The
lip of a bottle taps the edge of a glass. Out on the street, the snow
falls like a curtain of chaotic moths, and my name flashes across the
man's back as he heads out into the night.

It's still the same room, but now under the glow of the bulb my
father lies facedown on the floor. A shadow crosses his body. A
man steps to the front door. He stops. He steps back, pulls the
pint of whiskey from my father's hand and slowly stretches both
of my father's arms to the side. The man pulls the right cuff over
my father's hand, tugs slowly, and like a bird's wing the jacket lifts
off my father's arm, up and over his shoulders, as the man strips
the other sleeve down off my father's arm and hand. He holds
out the jacket, chest high, shakes it. He looks at the name. *¿Qué
va?* he mouths quietly. He laughs, swings the jacket softly like a
torero ready with his cape for the perfect *pase*, and in one quick,
light flick of his wrists he shrugs the jacket on. He opens the front
door. There is the sudden sound of wind, snow hitting the rusty
handrails on the steps, and then the distinct snap of buttons. He
walks down the steps into the swirling snow, crosses the sidewalk
and walks under the streetlights and the falling snow, pulls up the
jacket's collar, my name mixing with the light and the snow to
become something like memory.

It's a circle of men in a vacant space of tamped-down dirt next to a package liquor store. Five-thirty on a Friday and the men have punched out of the Roytype typewriter factory, have cashed their checks, and now here they are alongside this red brick liquor store, where, against its outer wall, they throw dice, yell out numbers, cheer and groan as the dice land in the dirt. Some men leave with empty pockets, others with a thick roll of bills clenched in their hands or tucked into their shirt pockets.

Dice, gambling, and chance traveled with Puerto Rican men wherever they went to work, became just as much a part of their work as their sweat or a cut hand. In Niles my father was wild with drink but his gambling days seemed behind him. There was no numbers in Niles. No dice. But all it took was for some new man to arrive, say, someone's long-lost cousin, someone traveling between San Francisco or Chicago to the East Coast, or a man fresh out prison, and in the back of the Puerto Rican House, where the grass had disappeared and the dirt was hard, the men gathered in a circle, scattered money within, and threw the dice against the side of the concrete steps. *¡Wepa! ¡No! ¡Dame el número, Raphi!* The surge of breath, the rising of bodies, the palpable feeling of blood pumping in a rush as the men shifted, looked with hard expectations as the dice rolled in the dirt and revealed their black numbers. The men yelled with triumph or dejection. My father, crouched down, his butt touching his heels, shook the dice in his hands like a maraca and flung them in the air.

Maybe one night it was the last thing he could bet. It was easy to move the sparse furniture against one wall, and then they had a smooth floor and empty wall. Dice in hand, my father felt the sure digits pulsing in his fingers, a seven or an eleven, and heard the dice click on the wall, tumbling slowly in a white-and-black blur, his heels suddenly numb when the yelling was not for him. Two dead bones still on the floor. The jacket held no weight when he handed it over. More than anyone else in the room he heard the strong burst of wind roaring through the trees, the sharp, long whistle of a train heading west across the river, and then the jacket's bright metal snaps being pinched together one after the other, so similar to the click of the dice as he shook them in his palm. That new man, wherever he was from, wherever he was going, walking out into the snowy night with a pocket full of money, the bright, sweet burn of whiskey on his tongue, his shoulders and arms warm inside the jacket, and his steps quick with luck, the luck of the dice and the road, and for this one night, walking with the luck of my name.

Who knows where my father lost the jacket. All I have is my memory: the turquoise truck, and as the unknown man drives down Main Street I say good-bye.

Memory darkens to nothing as if all the power at the Ready Theatre was cut off, the marquee lights died, and God had taken away the dusk. I might have briefly grimaced or smiled, let out a tight-lipped laugh. Perhaps bowed my head. Good-bye. There was no one there to talk to, no one to hear me. No one saw me. Good-bye. I didn't cry. I don't remember where I was headed. The night is gone. The days following don't return. I'm certain there was never a time when I told anyone I saw the man in the jacket. *Hey, Mom, remember how Chago lost my jacket? I saw some guy on Main Street wearing it.* Conversations like that never happened—life was too rushed, my mother up early and on the road for work, gone all day ten miles away in another state, arriving home late in the evening. My father too often drunk, filled with inexplicable rage, down the road on some trip or asleep on the couch. The jacket, finally, was forgotten, lost forever. Like my father's drinking, it was nothing to talk about. There were more important matters: work and paying bills.

Good-bye.

All I could do was get up every morning, slip on an old jacket, and walk to school. And wait. Wait for the inevitable. One day someone would see this man with a bushy mustache and work-stained hands, and though the gold letters on my jacket would be darkened by grease, frayed from rubbing against metal, they would recognize the name and say, *Hey, I saw this guy. He was driving a truck filled with junk. Is that your father?*

The kitchen begins to brighten in the early morning light. Draped over a chair in front of a steaming bowl of oatmeal is a blue jacket. It's not my jacket; it's a darker blue, not as shiny, and without the white stripes. It's as if my jacket has returned, though, and I decide immediately my father will never wear it again. Later, sitting on my bed, the jacket spread over my knees, I look closely at the letters, my index finger following the stitching around each one. In between each letter there are the barely discernable holes where a needle had punctured the fabric. Underneath my name, like a diaphanous shadow, is another name. I trace it and recognize it as belonging to a young man who lost control of his car, swerved off the road, and flipped over. I had attended the young man's wake out of respect for my mother's sister, who was his girlfriend. My mother must have bought the jacket from my aunt, or maybe she gave it to her. I can easily imagine my mother with scissors and a razor blade removing the young man's name and then trying her best to sew on the new letters so no one would know the difference. It's the best my mother can do. I can't refuse it. (His last name began with *B*, right next to *A*, so it must've been meant to be.)

At first I wear it occasionally. Then, no longer remembering where it came from, I wear it more and more, and just as my body grew, naturally the jacket became mine. Sometimes, though, I'd feel—in the rain, in the falling snow, in a strong wind—the slight weight and imprint of the letters across my shoulders, letters within letters, a name within a name, like blue in green.

Farmer's Creek

I was twelve years old, soon to turn thirteen, my hands covered in blood. We worked with knives at a rickety picnic table under an Indian summer sky. Abraham and I had just cleaned fifteen chinook salmon. I was in shorts, my thighs sticky with mud and scales and small orange eggs. When we left the creek the fish were stacked like a bundle of firewood in the back of the station wagon, and now—sliced open from tail to gills, their innards pulled out, their insides rinsed and rubbed by thumb until pink shiny clean—they lay five apiece in black garbage bags, ready for Abraham's family's deep freeze.

That fall my father had moved to Chicago. One day, on the phone, my mother talked of all the fish we were catching. He told her we should visit and he could sell them. Abraham and his father—Mr. Rodriguez wasn't working at the time—gave me four or five bags. In my mother's yellow Volkswagen Bug we drove the salmon across three state lines, and though it was wrong, probably illegal, in my young boy's mind I imagined an adventure: a chance to get out of Niles, walk the streets and avenues of Chicago, and make some new money. Only once did I question what we were doing. Stopped at a tollbooth, just before crossing into Illinois. My mother took too long digging into her purse before she dropped coins into the attendant's waiting hand. My stomach crazy with butterflies. When my mother let out the clutch, the engine stalled, coughed, and jerked forward throwing my head against the seat. The Bug chugged through the tollbooth, we were on our way again, everything okay.

I wonder what my mother remembers of that drive. We never talked about it. Maybe I became anxious because my mother worried the whole way, and maybe she turned to me as we approached the tollbooth and said, *Hope they don't ask to see what's in the trunk.* She would have smiled, maybe chuckled after her words. I see her excited for the trip, in her face the same adventure I imagined (how boring Niles must have been, my father one day simply gone, her driving to work in Indiana, returning to our quiet house). I want to remember my mother offering me a new experience, a chance to see my father in a different life, living in Chicago away from his drinking.

My father's eyes were clear and steady, his thick black hair neatly cut and combed back off his forehead, his mustache trimmed, and when he smiled his eyes no longer held regret and anger, and his lips were no longer set off by the sad parentheses of his droopy mustache. His dimples were deep, and his cheeks red. Change suited him. He liked to take us downtown, near Marshall Field's, where we'd window-shop in the stripes of light falling through the El's tracks. There was always someone playing a saxophone or trumpet with an upside-down hat filled with dollar bills and glinting coins, and the stripes of light and shadows became piano keys I stepped on, one long step after another, as I listened for the bell and the conductor's voice announcing the station. On the corner there was a storefront with two picture windows. My father would stop, point, his eyes full of wonder. Through one window I watched as a man in a flour-dusted apron spread tomato sauce in circles around a wide piece of dough. He sprinkled handfuls of cheese on top of the sauce, gently tossed on disks of pepperoni and slices of sausage, and then slid the pizza into a deep oven with a long-handled paddle. Just around the corner, through the other window, jagged flames and steam rose from blackened grills. A man turned a fat-marbled steak that looked too wide to fit on a plate. The smell of sizzling beef and baking dough made my stomach drop and roll, my jaws tingle. My father would say, *One day, one day we'll try.* He'd look at me. *And what would you want—pizza or steak?* And from underneath the thundering train, on the edge of the honking cars zooming along the avenue, it was thrilling to yell, *Both!*

Or he'd take us into the neighborhood by his sister's house and we'd shop at the markets. He and my mother picked out yuca, plantains, garlic, cilantro, rice, *gandules*, some pork chops or a roast. They'd stop at a bakery for coffee and a sweet pastry. Back at my aunt and uncle's brownstone, we'd have a nice Sunday dinner before we left my father in Chicago.

That was the father I liked best. I walk up to the third floor of the brownstone, enter the front room, walk through the living room and down the hall past the two flanking bedrooms and the bathroom, and stand in the middle of the kitchen. A curtain of orange and yellow beads hangs over a doorway. Behind the curtain is my father's room. I'm touching the beads of polished hard plastic. They click together as I grab them, slip my hand, arm, and shoulder through, and step past the curtain. There are four shelves on the right with cans and boxes of food, a large green tin of crackers, some colored plastic cups, and an oversized roasting pan. Beneath the last shelf there is a cot, a smooth pillow at its head, a white sheet and a red-and-blue quilt turned down at the neck, just before the pillow. A pair of black work shoes on the floor next to the bed. A small window lets in a shaft of light. When I look along the edge I can see endless blue sky. Everything is tidy and uniform, almost perfect.

When my father rose in the mornings, he probably needed to duck to miss the shelf. Maybe he sat on the edge of the bed with a cup of coffee. Maybe he thumbed through a newspaper. I wonder what he thought about, how he imagined his day, what he wanted or dreamed or hated. When he looked out the window, what did he see?

That was the father I liked best. He never said he missed us. During our visits there wasn't much talk about his being away, when he might come back, nothing about his room. I loved the newness, the order and cleanliness, the light from the window. I was drawn to the quiet privacy I imagined: lying in bed, watching the light glint—orange, red, yellow, purple-blue—in the beads, their colors tinting the words I followed in a book. My father had become monastic to me, a saint, living in that cell, waking in the morning and quickly dressing, then off to a steady day of hard work. And, hopefully, later in the evening, after a short prayer, he achieved sleep without a drink. That is the father I liked best. There was nothing wrong with him in that big city, on those anonymous streets and avenues where he shared the world with me. The cool winds of fall scrubbed us clean, awakened and pure. For that one season he held the glory of the world in a face I loved to look at, a face I learned to hold still in memory, return to, over time, and read the faint lines.

I was only a boy, soon to turn thirteen, and there I was bringing my father some fish, showing the work I had done, trying to help make some money, and telling him that I too could become a saintlike worker. *Chago, it's me. I am your son.*

*_**

We were fishing on the small island just before the old US 31 bridge when a shore fisherman cast his line too far across the channel and his lead snaghook caught Abraham's father's calf. The treble hook went right through his knee-high rubber boot. At a clinic on Deans Hill Road, the doctor made a small incision, removed the hook, and closed it with a few stiches. It was a gray, cool day. Mr. Rodriguez would need new boots but for now repaired the punctured boot with a piece of black tape. Fishing for the day was done. But as we headed back toward the river and the turn toward home I saw the sign for Hipps Hollow Road. The name "Farmer's Creek" had been planted in my mind by an uncle who talked of salmon and trout migrating up the creek from the river, and I had talked about going there one day so we could see what it was like. When I called out, *There's Hipps Hollow Road–for the creek*, Abraham's father turned right.

We were northeast of Berrien Springs, close to Eau Claire, driving through hilly woods, fields of corn, and apple orchards. Down in the valley there was a small bridge with steel rails, and we pulled off the road and followed some muddy tire tracks into a clump of trees. Standing on the bridge we saw dead salmon floating in the gurgling creek, live ones rifling through the shallows. We walked a trail along the creek with a net and scooped up two or three chinook salmon, laid them in the back of the station wagon next to our rods, and headed home.

Growing up in Niles, Abraham Rodriguez was my one Puerto Rican friend. He had heard that I liked to fish and wanted to fish in Berrien Springs near the dam, where Abraham and his father often went. (Perhaps my father said something to his father.) One Friday evening he knocked on our front door with an invitation.

When I remember the days, months, and seasons of fishing, I always return to the fall and see a river full of chinook and coho salmon—a dark, murky dream where huge schools of salmon dart back and forth, each fish becoming a shimmering scale as the school merges into a gigantic salmon making its way through the currents until something in the river makes it scatter like leaves whirled up in a strong breeze. Back then there was a snagging season, and we used heavy tackle—stiff, short rods several inches thick down by the handle; reels that would hold fifty- to seventy-pound test line (line a fish couldn't break, so if you snagged your line you had no choice but to cut it); and a heavy chunk of lead with a number-two treble hook on each end. You cast out, reeled in quickly, stopped, and pulled the rod hard, the tip of the rod lowered toward the water, as you jerked the snag hooks through the river. With so many salmon swimming toward the dam, it didn't take long to snag the side or head of a fish, your jerking motion hooking the treble hooks, and then the fight was on.

Out on the river boats were spread four or five feet apart like a silver flotilla setting forth; the wall of the dam was like a factory street after work, man after man, shoulder to shoulder, dropping and casting their lines out into the river; and everywhere thin lines of green and blue arcing and descending, falling into the water like quickly drafted lines, a large spiderweb covering the river. Hooked salmon broke the surface, sometimes two or three feet into the air, dark footballs or silver plows. The currents were like the furrows in a field, and the salmon rose in the air as if they had struck a stone in the earth. Salmon jumped, men yelled *heeey*, followed by a splash. A salmon three or four feet long leapt in the sunlight, soared like some huge, fat bird, and then crashed into the bottom of a boat, crazily twisting against the aluminum to find its way back into the river, the thud echoing over the dam's spillway.

The first time I went fishing with Abraham and his father, I immediately endeared myself to them. A cold drizzle was falling, the river pocked and glittered from the rain. All quiet save the sound of water meeting water. I was focused, even possessed, watching the surface as I reeled in my line, jerked, felt my snaghook bumping on the bottom. I saw the river briefly open, quietly, and then a fish's head dipping up and down, mouthing the surface, then dropping below in a silver flash. I had grown up on the river, had no fear, and, pulled by some instinct I stepped in. Some five or six feet offshore, I grabbed the fish, hooking two fingers underneath its quivering gills, and dragged it in. It still had some kick to its tail and lay against the sandy, pebble-strewn beach silver and purple splashed with brilliant greens and reds, its undersides snow white. It was a beautiful steelhead trout of five or six pounds. Abraham screamed with excited disbelief. We bent down and looked more closely. Under its mouth, a bit past its gills, someone had cut out a jagged square of flesh, the edges of the square already turning brown. Someone must've snagged the trout. I asked Abraham if he wanted it, he said of course. He was overjoyed to hold his first steelhead and became even more animated when he noted it was full of eggs. I was wet, would soon be cold, but I could see in Abraham's smile that I was all right. I could go fishing whenever I wanted.

After my father had been arrested several times for drunk driving, his sister and brother-in-law made him an offer: he'd move to Chicago, find work, and sober up. He and my mother were constantly fighting. He was drunk more than sober. He often missed work and was laid off. They still struggled with money, and his drinking hadn't slowed down. The arrests finally scared him. And with his driver's license suspended, he was going to have a hard time finding work in Niles. In Chicago he might have another chance. When he decided to accept his sister's offer, I never thought of that time as a separation between my mother and father. I never thought that it would create a greater distance between us, a wound that would never fully mend.

Niles was a small town. I was ashamed that my father was Puerto Rican. I didn't have a language to control what that might mean, and there was a trembling fear and silence in my stomach I couldn't understand. My father was not an insurance salesman, a lawyer, the owner of a lumberyard, or a teacher. He picked apples. He worked in factories for low wages. He was one of a handful of Puerto Rican men who came in the 1960s to work at the Green Giant mushroom cannery. He floundered there in the middle of nowhere, and drink became his only solace, kept him from drowning. Every time I was with him—going to the store, driving around town, at the barbershop on a Saturday—I was afraid someone would see me with my father. One afternoon on his way home from a bar he paused on the corner across from the police station to catch his breath after walking up the hill. Ignoring the traffic light he continued toward home, zigzagging across the street. When he reached the other side, my father was arrested. For weeks I walked the halls at school with my head held down. I could feel the shame and silence growing in my stomach, and I wondered if I curled inward even more, if I might find something—anything—on the other side. I couldn't dare to look at the newspaper and the thin, cramped lines of the police report that I was sure everyone else would read and remember.

We became poachers that fall because we scooped salmon from the creek with a long-handled fishnet or grabbed their tails with our hands. We chased them in the shallows until they grounded on a sandbar where we could grab their withering, sleek bodies and toss them up into the weedy bank. Or we chased them back and forth, up and down the creek, until we cornered a fish against a cut bank and the exhausted salmon floated gently into the net we held behind its broad tail. There was always much rifling and splashing of water, and though Abraham and I were often wet, it was the salmon twisting—eel-like, through as little as two inches of water on the pebbled edges of sandbars, or over a small dam of rocks—that burst the water clear and loud. The speed of salmon in and out of the creek was marvelous; they were quicksilver, sprinting at speeds I had never seen before.

We knew that scooping the salmon from the creek with a net was illegal but rationalized, whether true or not, that fishing for salmon with tackle would be okay. So we put together fly rods with spinning reels spooled with six- or eight-pound test, and for lures used Little Cleo and KO Wobbler spoons. When I found a salmon holding steady, still for a moment in the current or lying down in a gray hole, I walked a few feet ahead of the fish, tossed in my spoon, and let the current carry it—the line tight—up to the salmon's nose, the spoon shining orange and silver. Somewhere I had read that once salmon had traveled this far into their journey—here to the waters of their birth—they were no longer hungry; they only returned to lay their eggs, fertilize them, and die. All around—on the sandbars, floating upside down under submerged tree limbs, twisted within a gnarled driftwood snag, lying up in the tall grasses and fallen leaves—dead salmon were decaying, covered in white spots, nicks, and cuts, some with chunks of flesh torn out, fins cracked or missing, their eyes gouged out by some bird, or their tails gnawed down to bone and cartilage (the night work of a 'possum, raccoon, or coyote). I'm not sure if it was instinct or rage that drove the salmon to strike—but they struck hard, lightning quick. The water clear, clean, the fine sand of the creek's bottom blondish beige. A salmon, suspended in the current with such form and power, its lean body flexing, its tail moving back and forth like a silk flag, my spoon tumbling in a slow revolution, the barbs on the treble hooks sharp in the afternoon light gathering below the creek's surface. The hard jerk in my hand running up my arm as I pulled back and set the hook, the creek exploding with the salmon breaking the surface then running to shallow water to try and lose the spoon against the bottom.

Every strike was a marvelous reversal of being: I became the salmon and set the hook out of some mysterious instinct or excitement to strike.

It never took long to land a fish. They were already exhausted from their journey. Unless the fish was able to run down into some tree roots and break the line, there were a few fine minutes of fighting as it ran up and down the creek, jumped in the air, and tried to dive deep into a hole. The challenge, with our rods and light lines, was to keep the salmon close, not to let it run too far downstream. Sometimes a fish pulled us along the bank and we had no choice but to follow its frenzied run for life.

Although what we were doing was wrong, Abraham and I were not as bad as the hunter who one day stopped on the bridge, pulled his twelve-gauge shotgun from his truck, and from the middle of the bridge unloaded as many shells as he could into a school of salmon. We knew our fishing would never make it into the pages of *Outdoor Life*, *Fur, Fish & Game*, or *Esquire*, but it was all the sport we had. Two young boys ten miles down the road from home. Boys growing up poor, boys who would soon go to work, boys with unanswered questions about their fathers, their lives.

Our fishing was serious. Abraham and his father took the fish home to their family, and I too had a desire to bring some fish home. On those days when we left empty-handed, the creek murky and fast after a hard night's rain, we were downcast and defeated, and sometimes I glimpsed anger tightening Abraham's jaw. We could never just drive to Berrien Springs to go fishing; we had to consider the gas money. Some days, it seemed there was plenty of money (I often had a few dollars to contribute). Other days,

Abraham and I returned bottles we picked up along the road to buy a gallon of gas.

When I look back on our times on that creek I experience a sense of wonder because we knew what we were doing, we knew how to find and catch the fish, and with their beautiful struggle those salmon, even if for only a moment, helped me escape my life. And there was something in their journey from Lake Michigan, up the St. Joe River, and all the way to Farmer's Creek that I longed to understand. They traveled far and wide and deep into Lake Michigan for three or four years as they grew long and fat, and then one late-summer day they left and began their return. In all that water there was a life where time did not exist on a clock or a calendar, the migrating salmon and trout reading currents, sands, rocks, shorelines, winds, and light as they returned to their streams, their origins. Theirs was a story of memory and migration much like mine. My father, Abraham's father, had both migrated to begin working in Michigan, where I was born. *Three Rivers*: a most pleasant sounding name, my birthplace. I imagined I was a part of the salmon's water memory, part of the migration and story they lived.

They migrated in waves—first the chinook salmon, followed by the coho salmon, their sides turning more apple red as the fall passed, and then the lake trout followed the salmon, as did the steelhead and brown trout, because they ate the salmon eggs. We would fish Farmer's Creek from September through December, following different fish as they entered the creek in thick waves that slowly thinned out into a small trickle.

Over time Abraham and I became more excited by trout fishing, especially catching the sleek and ferocious steelheads, which loved to jump, to run deep and long. We learned to cure salmon eggs with Borax. With scissors we'd cut small colored gauze squares, drop four or five eggs in each, and tie up a small bag with thread. Or we would cure a whole sack of eggs with Borax in a Ziploc bag, the smell becoming more and more rank as we cut off pieces, pierced our treble hooks through the floury membrane, and cast it out into the currents. We learned to work with sponges—neon-glow pink, orange, yellow, and green—that we cut into small pieces and simmered in a mix of anise flavoring, water, and Vaseline. We would roll them around in more Vaseline and keep them in a jar or a plastic tub, and on the river pull a single hook through the sponge. We no longer fished the island or riverbanks down by the bridge but instead joined the long line of men on the concrete wall next to the dam, the water flowing out white and fast when the floodgates were open, the trout leaping in silvery arcs quoting the air before the falls.

September and October and November spilled by as we followed the fish migration. Abraham stood on the wall fighting a steelhead, slowly walking down to the end, and I, some twenty-five feet below, bent over the river and netted his trout, lifting it onto the bank.

It's difficult to admit I was happy my father was gone. It's almost like saying I'm happy my father was an alcoholic, I'm happy you were arrested for drunk driving, I'm happy you went away to live in Chicago. It's like saying, *I hated you.*

For once I had no anxiety, no dread, no crazy cutting butterflies in my stomach. He could no longer yell at me (or my mother). He could no longer stumble around the house drunk looking for something to do (painting a fence, fixing some door that he had punched a hole through, working on a friend's car). He could no longer hit me, tell me how stupid or useless I was, or embarrass me. There were days I couldn't eat, when my stomach trembled with a sore nervousness, and my shoulders and arms always felt like they were on the verge of beginning to shake uncontrollably. I became withdrawn and quiet, afraid that I might come home and find my father asleep on the couch, wake him up, and then have to take his rage.

When my father left for Chicago I was immediately free. Slowly the pain in my stomach subsided, the years of fear fell away, and I no longer obsessed over what I might've done wrong to deserve his anger. A great weight lifted from my shoulders, my arms calmed, and I tried to walk with my head held high, to follow the swaying trees, the blue sky, the glinting river down the hill from our house.

*
**

I am a boy again. I dip a net behind a fish and lift it from the water without thought—just there, my hands wet—the trout and I are one.

*
**

I will always remember Abraham's father fishing in his green plastic helmet, the helmet men wore at the Green Giant cannery. When they worked in the bunker-like growing houses, they attached a light to the front of the helmet so they could see the mushrooms growing in the wet, dark soil.

*
**

I see them often in memory's fenestra, still and silent as if cut in colored glass. The Puerto Rican House: a gray two-story duplex where the men came to drink, talk, and tell stories. Brilliant illustrations of childhood.

A man leaning against a black aluminum porch column, one leg crossed behind the other, his arms folded over his white guayabera, a fedora cocked on his head covering his eyes, a cigarette dangling from his lips. A man sitting on a weathered fruit crate, legs wide, crooked hands clasping his knees. The roar of laughter. Two or three crinkled paper bags holding tall cans of beer or pints of rum standing on the concrete porch.

Whenever we left, or came home, they were watching, Third Street becoming a border of the visible and invisible, the watcher and the watched, the remembered and the forgotten. Whatever stories they shared, whatever jokes they laughed at, whatever memories of loss or hope they raised a drink for, whatever they said about my father, who no longer came over, who was no longer home, lived there on the street between our two front porches. Came to life in their watching. Came to life in that green plastic helmet.

*
**

Pieces of memory shatter, separate, and then rearrange themselves into a mosaic of stained glass, like fish scattering in currents and then schooling together in a pool below a dam. I find myself standing at the empty lot where the Puerto Rican House once stood. I linger in their incomplete lives—the chain-link fence, the tall grass and weeds, the gray cement stairs marooned in the middle of the lot. I don't remember Abraham's father ever standing on the porch, never saw him leaning against a column, a wrinkled paper bag in his hand. He once drank like my father. Unlike my father, he never stood on that porch. He never had to leave home.

He never mentioned or asked about my father being away. He took me fishing, he was passionate about it, and the way he talked, laughed, and looked at life was infectious. We are driving home through the twilight one day from Berrien Springs. Mr. Rodriguez's mood is high because we have several fish, and he sings along to the Rolling Stones' "Miss You" blasting from the radio, the windows down, the cold evening air rushing in, all the while sipping from a bottle of MD 20/20 wine. He notices a stream on the side of the road as if for the first time, the edges of the stream brimming with a thick green plant. He pulls over, his face filled with joy. The western sky above the stream strewn with broken clouds, the sky above the clouds blue with a few stars, and down near the treeline there's bright, soft pink light. Those will make a *chévere* salad, Mr. Rodriguez says, pointing to the stream. He gets out, walks to the stream, and returns with an armful of plants, roots dripping dirt and water. He gets in and lays the greens on the passenger side. He turns to us in the glow of the overhead light. *See*, he looks at Abraham and me, a big smile on his face. He tells us again it will make a delicious salad, *qué chévere*, with some vinegar and oil, and he keeps calling it a Spanish word—*berros, berros de agua?*—I cannot remember, only hear *barrels, barrels of water*. He asks me how you say it in English. I'm not sure. For some reason I have the image of small, crustless white bread sandwiches, clean and dainty on a bone-white plate. Along the edges of the bread there are waves of green. Something to go with afternoon tea. *Watercress sandwiches*. He hands us each a tendril of the plant, a soft vine with waxy small leaves shaped like spades. It's wet on my tongue, full of cold water as I bite down on the leaves and the vine, and immediately there's a burst of black pepper and lemon. I swallow and say, I think it's what they call watercress. And they make sandwiches from it. Ah, he says, repeating the word a few times, and then: *I will make salad tonight.*

My father and I stood in the alley outside the bar's back door. There was a dumpster, the ground littered with pieces of paper and cardboard, a silver trash can on each side of the black door, and a bell of gold light raining down from the tin-shaded green lamp overhead. My father had brought maybe ten or twelve of the salmon, still somewhat frozen. He stepped inside. I looked up and down at the ends of the alley, pewter blue squares of evening sky and street traffic, red brake lights winking from the passing cars. Through the door's porthole window the place looked empty. There was a long shiny bar, green and brown and clear bottles lit and reflected against a mirror, a square lampshade with horses or dogs on it hanging over a pool table, and all along the bar empty stools with red seats.

I heard laughter followed by muffled voices.

To accept his sister and brother-in-law's offer to live in Chicago, my father had to agree to no longer drink and to find work, which he did at a Bearcat plant. But here he was inside a bar, and when we walked there it was as if he already knew where he was going. The voices mingled with some music. A wave of chilled air drifted through the alley as the twilight faded. I walked to the end. Horns, revving engines, the *squeak-squeak-squeak* of worn-out brakes, the *whoosh* of cars going by in a glint of silver. The avenue bright with the liquid ink of neon dividing the shiny sidewalk and the darkening sky. The avenue went west forever, soft white clouds herding together on the horizon in the last bit of light. I walked down the avenue—nowhere to go, not wanting anything, not worried about my father coming out of the bar and looking for me. The sidewalk and the neon pulsed together, and I followed without purpose some energy or rhythm lost in all the windows I passed: shoe shops, bakeries, restaurants, and bars. It is a moment of memory that doesn't need any added significance. It's just a bustling, bright avenue in the twilight. I don't know how far I walked, or for how long. I stop. A young woman in a dark dress patterned with colorful paisleys lifts a tray from the end of the bar over her shoulder, the green bottles of beer beading cold, her white apron briefly separating from the pleated skirt of her dress, and I listen—whether I hear it or not through the window—as her black heels strike the wood-planked floor.

My father leaned against a brick wall at the end of the alley, his hands inside the pockets of his windbreaker, the collar pulled up. He smiled, gave me a wave, his hand fat with rolled-up bills. The next day my father and uncle went out again with a bag of salmon. In two days my father sold them all. When my mother and I returned to Niles, the first thing we did was stop at Abraham's house. I knocked on the screen door. A moment later there was a hand pulling the curtain away from the small window on the inside door. Abraham's father. I told him we sold them all, handed him the money. Maybe $100, maybe $125. I told him that my mom had taken out some gas money. His smile broad and white, his chuckle exuding something more than thanks, his eyes lighting up, his brown face tinted red. Now it seems like such a small amount, paltry to some (a couple goes out to dinner, orders a cheap bottle of wine, skips the appetizer or dessert, and they have enough to pay the check), but for that family of six, when Abraham's father wasn't working, it must have been more than welcome.

Months would pass and he'd still talk with wonder about the money. But I never understood why he didn't ask about selling the salmon again. It's not just a missing memory. I think now that it has more to do with who Mr. Rodriguez was, how he lived his life. He would never ask. Maybe the money was enough. Maybe in times of need we are fortunate to receive just the thing to keep us going. Maybe we learn not to ask from others but to live and believe anything is possible.

Later that fall Abraham's father would get a job with the city on the snowplowing and street repair crew. This was the kind of job, back then, that one would die for. Good pay, benefits, job security. Mr. Rodriguez became almost Zen-like in his appearance, actions, and words—I loved to hear him talk in Spanish and English, watch his face: the high cheekbones, his salt-and-pepper mustache, and his beautiful brown skin and silver hair. He was an intense and yet calm man, and he came to possess an even greater assurance when he started that job and quit drinking. I can still see the elegance of his clean gray slacks tucked into his knee-high rubber boots, and the strength in his dry, strong, bony hands gripping his fishing rod or a shovel.

*
**

My father did not stay in Chicago for long. He came home and started drinking again with a passion. Mr. Rodriguez knew he was back. There was no reason to ask about selling salmon.

*
**

Our last time on Farmer's Creek, Abraham and me, a bright December day. The trees puffy with soft snow, the creek sparkling, and all around us the woods and fields glittering in silver and blue, the sky high and endless. Abraham was now sixteen and drove us when we went fishing. He seemed quiet, often preoccupied, even angry, and the three main subjects he approached repeatedly were school, work, and sex. There was often a question about what I thought about so-and-so, or how he wanted to be a part of such-and-such team and become a star. Because he could now drive he was going to find a job. And soon he needed his own place where he could bring women. Then what did I think about so-and-so, always a blonde girl at school, and everything he would love to do with her. I could only shake my head, smile, try to follow along as he talked with animated passion.

That last time we couldn't find any fish in the creek. We hiked farther north away from the river, miles we had never walked before. Snow swooshing from our steps, the murmur of the creek. The land started to rise and we followed the trail up a ledge. There were many pine trees thick with snow, and the wind picked up for a moment and sent the snow drifting from the trees, powdery and mesmerizing like a miniature storm. The snow, the trees, and the ground glowed with an underlying blue, and in between the spaces of the bare trees layered with snow the sun turned the air golden.

Abraham stopped. He shushed me with his finger. We had neon orange sponges on our lines, a few split shots above. He unhooked his sponge from his fishing rod and pulled out a bit of line. He pointed. Down below a sagging pine branch there was a small pool surrounded by currents and filled with sunlight. Abraham flipped his rod and released a splendid cast near the overhanging tree. The sponge glided down and caught in the current, darted, drifted, and slowly floated into the pool. There was a quick shadow in the pool, Abraham yelled after he set the hook, *I got him*, and raised his rod high over his shoulder, the rod bending in a sharp *C*, the sea blue filament taut. And then, in what seemed like only seconds, a green fish flipped, tumbled—green white, green white—at our feet. It breathed big gulps of air, the loveliest shades of green running from its head along its spine and side to its white belly. When Abraham lifted it toward the sun there was a wide streak of red. It had one black spot just past the gill near its eye, and then barely visible trout spots along its back and fins. It was so clean, so fresh and cold looking, and so remarkably green. We had no idea what kind of fish it was or what it was doing so far up the creek. We wondered aloud if it was possible for a fish to travel this far. We agreed it wasn't a steelhead. Definitely wasn't a jack salmon. Abraham thought it might be some cross species, some trout we had never seen, or maybe just a big rainbow. I remember Abraham lifting the fish high toward the sky, the flash of sharp snow, the green shadow of the trout outlined in gold, and the murmuring creek calling for me to remember its faint music.

*
**

In a dusty migrant shack there's a bare, stained mattress on the floor. Light falls through the cracks in the wall. My father and the other men are talking in the shade of a cottonwood tree. Through the open door I see the wind pick up, washing the leaves in August light. I lie in the room's cool shadows before we head back out into the fields. In my back bedroom the electric heater is running. I sprint across the room and jump under the covers, the sheets like the ice on the window next to my bed. I rent a single-room cottage on Mesa Road. I have a café table pushed to the window. There's an open notebook, a pen resting in its spine. Thick fog drifts in off the Pacific and I follow its graceful arms as it winds its way through the field and embraces the cypress trees. Room after room of memory. My father's room is the center of them all. Down the hall, just off the kitchen, right behind that colorful beaded curtain. What did he feel in that room after a long day of work when the lights went out, the apartment quiet, the only sound a spring on his bed creaking as he turned toward the wall, some streetlight falling through the window too white and loud across his eyes? When I stood there in his room at the age of thirteen, I never imagined that I might one day become a writer, that I might want my own small, silent room, a lonely room where anything is possible. Even in a room as small as a pantry there can be the purest of mornings.

I stand just past the threshold and take in the room's lack of space and objects—the bed, the cans of beans, the twenty-pound sack of rice on its side on the lowest shelf, the large tin of thick crackers—all mute, eternal, still waiting for me to carry them into my life. Sometimes I'm in the kitchen, looking through the yellow and orange beads again, the curtain like a window screen. I make out cans of condensed milk, a bag of Café Bustelo, a jar of Tang. Ammonia, Clorox, and Pledge are on the highest shelf next to a tin bucket. On the bottom shelf with the sack of rice is a votive candle with the figure of Saint James, the patron saint of laborers, emblazoned on the glass. The candle is red, the lip of the glass blackened by the candle's flame, Saint James in a green cloak, standing on the prow of his boat, ready to reach the shore and begin saving souls. Down below the shelf there's a pillow with the soft imprint of my father's head. I search in the light and shadows for something of who he was—Santiago, Saint James, Chago, my father—working in a factory, bending in a field, walking down an avenue, seated on a train, out on some road making his way home.

Sown in Earth

We stood in the middle of the pier looking out on the blue freshwater sea. My father was very thin, his guayabera and freshly pressed black pants elegant in the sun, and there was something peaceful in his bony, gnarled hands holding the pier's rails, as if he were vacationing. A few boats bobbed on the white-crested waves. The people on the beach tiny and distant, yet I could easily make them out: sitting on colorful blankets and sheets, children building castles and running along the shore, and everywhere splashing in the rising and falling waves.

My father would have been about thirty-seven, and even though he had shaved closely that morning, his face smooth and clean and lean, he had missed those glittering gray and silver hairs just at the ends of his sideburns.

The wind picked up and a sheet of heavy clouds moved in from the southwest, the July air turning hotter, the sky blanketed by a dulling haze.

My father rested his chin on the palm of his hand, his elbow leaning on the guardrail. Lately, he had taken to having my mother drive us thirty miles from Niles to St. Joe so he could walk out on the pier and look at the freshwater sea, Lake Michigan.

The sea stirred with the breeze, the blue water pocked with discs of gold. My father seemed lost, as if by staring into the horizon he vanished and became the waves, crested and bobbed, disappeared, and reappeared out there in the blue.

My father hardly ever talked to me, and from about the time I was nine he never seemed to want to talk in English, and there arose between us a great distance like a turbulent sea I didn't know how to cross. He had lost his job at a factory. I'm not sure if it was because of cutbacks or his drinking. He had been arrested again for drunk driving. Given his previous offenses, he had to serve time in a program that allowed him to work and stay at home during the week, but on Friday nights he had to check into the county jail in St. Joe for the weekend. He became even more silent, and we each began to live within our own loneliness.

I looked out at the horizon, tried to find the spot my father searched for. There were mythical days young people here waited for, days that never seemed to arrive. A high, clear blue summer sky. One stood on the lake shore, or better yet, looked from the vantage point of a high bluff or a tall dune, and then the Chicago skyline—ninety miles away—rising out of the freshwater sea, the buildings forming like black boxes on the horizon, the straight line and pointed top of the Sears Tower making it all the more alive. I couldn't see it—there were the waves, the warm wind on my arms, the white clouds, the horizon, but no distant buildings, no sudden realization of things arising out of nothing. But maybe my father knew of those days. Maybe, at times, he dreamed them, and so up on the bluff behind us, when he had spent his Saturdays and Sundays in the county jail, maybe there was some small window he knew, and on a clear day he had a way of looking I may one day discover.

My sister and mother walked toward us. My father waved for us to follow, and we all walked back toward the shore and then to the car. My father sat in the passenger seat while my mother drove. The countryside unfolded in gold and green and blue, the darker shapes of the orchards coloring with ripe apples and plums and peaches. Without saying a word, almost as if by instinct, my mother pulled off the highway into Vollman's Market.

There's the smell of cantaloupe and dust mixing in the warm air drifting in through the pole-barn doors that I can't seem to lose, that places me there in that fruit-tinged air. I see tomatoes, zucchinis, mounds of green beans piled on tables, and on three fifty-five-gallon drums set side by side, their tops covered by a red-and-white-checkered cloth, there are quart-size cardboard baskets filled with fat blueberries. The cantaloupes are in a small pyramid. Bushel baskets are filled with red and gold apples, and the baskets are on pallets. Fruit flies fill the air. There are cellophane packages of dried fruit and nuts on the table next to the cash register along with jars of red, deep purple, and orange preserves. Against the wall a set of clear coolers are filled with gallons of milk and sodas and eggs and butter.

A woman straightened ten-pound bags of potatoes on a pallet, the sound of the thick paper crunching as she pulled on a bag, lifted, and dropped it into the pattern she was making, the smell of wet, beginning-to-rot potatoes stinging my nose. I stood there for a moment. Then she turned to me and straightened up. She was short, heavy, with black hair and glasses. I asked her about a job. Most of the work, she told me, was picking corn and some odd work around the market, helping to unload deliveries, sweeping and cleaning, maybe helping to pick and bag potatoes. She suddenly yelled over to an older man (the concrete floor was splotched with dark stains, and suddenly I felt a spasm of shame deep in my stomach as I flicked away a green fly crawling down my arm). The man, who was her husband and the owner of the market, came over. She told him I was interested in work. He had a thick, bristly mustache turning gray, his hands and arms trembling with a slight tick as he stood there, and it was hard to see his eyes because of his green hat, the bill pulled down low. He simply said, *That'd be fine*, after looking me over a bit, and like his wife he mentioned picking corn and the extra work of loading and unloading trucks, some cleaning, bagging potatoes. I turned and looked across the market at my mother, sister, and father standing behind a table of lettuce, and behind them the open doors and the cars passing by on their way north.

And my father? Can he work too?

Mr. Vollman tipped the bill of his hat back. He and his wife looked past me across the market, their eyes not widening but their faces filling with some strange recognition. They looked at each other, as if they were used to talking without ever saying a word, and then she said, *Yes, your father can work too. We'll see you both here tomorrow morning at six.*

Returning to that summer I have a difficult time pinpointing the exact year—conflicting memories of work, drink, and those long, unending, sickening days when getting sober meant sitting with my hate and loss, are what return to me. That summer must have been in 1982, when I was fourteen. I'm not sure why I asked about the job. When I close my eyes I see the black-and-orange Help Wanted sign tacked to a thick cottonwood tree as we pulled into the dusty driveway, the sign's squared perfection and how it seemed to float there upon the black-and-green tree. I don't remember my father mentioning the sign, and I don't remember him asking about the job. In my memory—as I recall that day becoming grayer with thick, wet clouds, my father trying to sober up after a three-month bout with drink, the quiet stillness of the market save for a small fan blowing by the cash register, and then the rattling glass as my father tried to steady his hand and the bottle he lifted from the cooler—the feeling for my remembrance tells me he hadn't said a word. I asked about the job because I had always worked in some way (paper routes, detasseling corn, picking blueberries) and I felt the money would be helpful.

In that one moment when I turned, saw gnats drifting back and forth in the gold, dusty light falling on the fruits and vegetables, I turned because I felt something rise in me, because I remembered my father, turned to find him, and then asked if he could work too.

There was an odd chill in the market. I looked outside, the sky predicting rain. We headed from the market, my father drinking his ginger ale, my sister and mother eating peaches.

What feeling rose in me I don't know. Apology, perhaps, as if I could let my father know that though we never talked about his weekends in jail, I never thought to blame or hold it against him. Yes, I had to apologize because on those weekends I was happy not to worry about him being drunk at home. Happy he had to go away. Happy he had those weekends in jail.

We passed the cottonwood tree, and when my father opened his door I pointed at the sign on the tree and said, *They gave me a job.* Everyone looked at my extended arm for a moment, almost as if my words had come from my hand, and then I asked my mother if she could drive me out here in the morning before she went to work.

They're paying $4.35 an hour, I said, and thought how it was a good amount above minimum wage. And I asked if Chago could work too.

My mother said, *Yes, I'll bring you out.*

There was no more discussion, no questions asked as we got into the car, nor as we drove home. Once home my mother and father put together lunches for the next day. My father pulled a scotch plaid thermos from below the kitchen sink. He raised it next to his ear, shook it, listened for broken glass. I never heard whatever he heard in his shaking; a gust of wind hit the side of the house, a branch striking the roof crazily, and out past my mother's and father's darkened profiles the sky turned blue-black, then silver sparks of rain shattered against the windowpane. My mother turned from the counter and placed two bowls, each with a spoon inside, on the table. She placed a coffee cup next to each bowl. In the morning we'd have oatmeal and coffee, and in that darkening kitchen of summer rain I knew the morning would arrive soon.

My decision to ask about the job was weighted by memory. Perhaps the summer before (or the summer before that) my mother's brother had returned to town and was looking for work. He, my father, and I had driven out into the hot August fields of Berrien County. Driving along those long roads flanked by fields and orchards, they would turn onto dusty one-lane roads that led into migrant camps of small green or white shacks, children standing in the hard sun or running under dust-covered trees, and always the women hanging laundry—a bright confetti of colors—along precarious clotheslines. These camps were mostly inhabited by Mexican families, but back then, in the early '80s, we also drove through compounds of three or four shacks inhabited by Haitian or Jamaican families. My father seemed free and easy—speaking either Spanish or his fast, musical English—in the camps. Usually, at first, the women would look at us strangely, but once my father began to talk they would tell us where we needed to ask about work, often a mile or so down the road on the edge of a field, where we would find a green or silver trailer. We never found work at any of those trailers; there were already too many workers, and in my memory I remember a kind of wonder in my father's voice when he said we could've worked at one farm, but we needed to bring our family and live in one of the shacks.

As I write these words and return to this colored geography of deep brown dirt, green crops and orchards, the rushing wind lifting my hair, I imagine some larger memory behind our driving out to the fields. My uncle, perhaps, asked my father to help him search for work because it was something my father was accustomed to doing all his life, and he did it well. When my mother and father moved to Michigan from Hartford, Connecticut, in the mid-'70s, my father had, in fact, found them—right away—work picking apples; and, of course, my parents met because my father came to Michigan to work.

I don't remember the first day or two of our work at Vollman's Market. What I do remember is the morning—gold, everything: the grass, the trees, a long clothesline speckled with dew—when my mother dropped us off at the market, and there in the driveway were three men. Two of them leaned against the hood of a long blue car, and the third man stood inside the open door of a cream-colored truck, his arms resting against the door. My mother stopped the car, looked at my father. After I stepped out of the car I recognized the men as my father's friends.

I suppose he'd told them that there was work (he must've easily understood that there was more than he and I could do, that they might ask for work too). When Mr. Vollman pulled up with the tractor and wagon to pick up my father and me, he didn't seem to look on the scene strangely. He shut down the tractor and jumped to the ground. He pushed the bill of his hat back and then took off his gloves as he approached. We all stood in a semicircle, Mr. Vollman in the middle. My father stepped forward, and in a voice of ease and confidence said (his arms spread wide at his sides), *They can work too.*

Mr. Vollman looked around briefly, looking each man in the face. And then he looked at me.

I'll always remember his smile, the twitch of his bushy gray mustache, and how he waved us all toward the wagon, and how we all jumped on the back, the sudden sound of talk and laughter, and how when the tractor hit the dirt lane and jerked, I was immediately aware of the cold morning air, the cornfields endlessly beautiful in the golden dew.

My sense of our work back then has become dull over the years. I never experience the deep-in-the-bones pain from that time, I never have those afternoons and nights of undisturbed sleep because sleep is what the pain in my arms and legs called for. The work comes back to me only in the weather: the fields cold and wet in the morning, and then by noon—my face red and cut by the sharp cornstalk leaves, my thighs raw and swollen from my soaked jeans rubbing between my legs as I stoop up and down in those tight lanes—the sun high and hot. The smell of the wet burlap sack at my side mixing with the smell of my sweat and wet clothes, and then an odd odor I can't seem to place but imagine as my skin rotting like the bruised, overripe fruits in the trash heap behind the market.

The work returns finally as a rhythm, a faint music: I follow it in the soft beat of a lightly tapped conga drum, the quick scratching tempo of shaking maracas, my hands pulling ears of corn from a stalk and sliding them into my burlap sack, my feet lifting slowly and coming down in light, giant steps that took me further down the row of corn toward the bright light at the end, as a new, quieter music arose within my thighs and spread up into my stomach, chest, and arms, a tender, invisible flutelike music that called me to work with it, to keep on moving, to not lose the music, to know that soon we'd be done.

The wagon piled higher and higher with the bags of corn we dumped there, and then eventually we jumped on the back and the tractor jerked up the lane and back to the market. Once there, we headed into the pole barn where there was a wagon filled with potatoes.

My father stepped up on an overturned milk crate, a shovel in his hands, and then placed his feet wide on the wagon as he began to drop the potatoes onto a running conveyor belt, the potatoes bouncing and nudging each other as they made their way down the line. One of my father's friends stood on the side looking for stones, plants, weeds, and bad-looking potatoes which he threw into a wooden box at his feet. At the end of the conveyor the potatoes gathered into a pool that continued to rise the longer my father shoveled potatoes. Another of his friends used his hands to scoop the potatoes from the pool into a scale, and once it was loaded with ten pounds, dropped the potatoes into a new open white bag, and then placed the bag on a waist-high table where another of my father's friends twisted the tops of each bag closed with a copper band. He lifted and tossed the bag free into the air toward me—I caught each bag in my cupped elbows, one of my hands immediately grabbing the bottom and the other forming around the twisted, copper-banded top. Twisting at the waist I laid it down on a pallet, twisted up and caught another, twisted, laid it down, beginning to create a three-by-five pattern, twisting and laying down, twisting and laying down, the pattern growing into the layered rows of ten-pound bags of potatoes I stacked on the pallet, the rising pattern of bags clean and new and vivid, the paper and copper bands etching themselves within the grain of my palm, and the pain of the work sometimes forgotten as I focused on the image of the red mountains and a thin green stream running between those mountains on the bags.

Later in the afternoon, under the high, cutting sun, we followed a potato picker rumbling through the dusty fields, a few of the men standing on the picker looking for stones and weeds while the rest of us picked up the potatoes that fell off the wagon and those that turned up in the picker's wake.

Right away I realized that I was not a man like my father or his friends. I could not keep up with them; I didn't have the body, experience, and memory of work most of them had had since childhood, my father beginning to work in the fields of Puerto Rico when he was eight or nine years old. Their bodies were like old books forgotten on a dusty shelf, and in the pages their muscle and sweat were the verbs and conjunctions that composed the truth of their lives. Bodies that never gave up, would never be erased because they faced that truth without too much complaint. I wish I could go back and share with them how I see them working in a field, how I read their lives in this old book. "Each morning you have to break through the dead rubble afresh so as to reach the living warm seed," Ludwig Wittgenstein remarks. Maybe I could share with them an image that, in a different way, expressed the same thing.

My father and his friends asked Mr. Vollman if we could go out to the edge of the potato fields, out back behind the market, and use one of the migrant shacks during our breaks between picking corn, bagging potatoes, and the afternoon potato picking. There were two out there, side by side, and although they seemed bright and clean and freshly painted white, I think they were the remnants of a time long past, a time when the market was a much bigger farm, when families had traveled to live here and work all summer and deep into the fall. My father and his friends picked up some of the still edible fruits and vegetables that had been thrown away, a few bruised peaches or a cantaloupe soft with rot yet still good on one side, some wet celery, a blackening onion. We walked the quarter mile or so out to the shack. Someone dug some potatoes from the field. Someone started a small fire of sticks within a ring of broken bricks and stones. The potatoes were peeled and washed in the spigot in between the two shacks and then boiled in an old pot on the fire. Someone had brought a small jar of mayonnaise and an off-white set of salt and pepper shakers, and the good parts salvaged from the celery and onion were chopped up, mixed with the cooked and cubed and salted and peppered potatoes and mayonnaise.

The warm potatoes melted the mayonnaise velvety smooth, the celery crunchy and briefly bitter, the onion burning the roof of my mouth and nose. I drank a cup of cold water from the spigot. The lunch felt like the end of the day, my body beginning to rest, content with those warm flavors deep in the pocket of my stomach, content in the quieting stillness of my arms and legs.

Inside the shack the walls were bare and brown, the smell of cracked and crumbling wood, the scent of wet soil and rain. A dusty mattress lay on the floor—stained by water or sweat or something I did not know. It felt cool and good to step out of the sun. I sat down on the mattress, entranced by that summer doorway, the square of gold and blue vividly present and real because of the darkness of the shack, and the talk and laughter of my father and the men outside. It became an original moment I couldn't—I still can't—frame; and now, just as then, I let it exist, as it needed to exist after a morning of cold, wet work. I lie back on the mattress, the gold and blue coloring the insides of my eyelids, as I fall into a deep colored sleep that, no matter how brief, is broken only when I hear the men call that it's time to go back to work.

Somewhere in the regions of my mind are the names of those men, my father's friends. When I close my eyes they all seem to blur together, leaning back against a pile of corn we've just picked, walking behind a wagon full of potatoes, their bodies like brown shadows in the drifting dust, their faces indistinct because of the sun and sweat in my eyes. Their names are nowhere to be discovered.

I recall an old man with a droopy long gray mustache, his eyes sharp silver-blue. His chin and his cheeks are speckled with silver and gray, and it seems he might have shaved every three or four days. I only heard him speak Spanish, yet his hair—a light sandy brown—is the longest I have ever seen a Puerto Rican man keep, striking the collar of his shirt. He always wears a very clean and neat white or light blue dress shirt. His dark blue pants attract dust, and considered alongside his shirt, I don't see a man ready to go to work but, instead, a man taking a stroll down a city street on his way to a park, where he'll sit on a bench and read a book in the company of pigeons and swaying trees. Almost as if when taken together these features don't create a definitive portrait of this man, and so I can see them only in the simplest of terms: the features of a man getting old and in need of money who worked in a field alongside other men who lived with similar circumstances, men he had worked with for at least five decades.

There is also a very dark man, and his face stands out because his eyes are coal black, his cheeks deeply defined as if chiseled into their smooth slenderness, and he has the wickedest smile, and each time he smiles I see a worn knife drawn across his lips, and then hear heavy laughter inhabited by cigarettes and something deep within him that he likes to share but will never give away. I have to remember his face the only way I can: *Asian*. An ancient face I've seen in museums on masks and figurines, and a face I've passed on the streets of New York, San Francisco, Madrid. And I seem to remember his face because his hair is the black of a raven's wing. His name—like all their names—remains a mystery. But he always wore, no matter how hot, a green plastic helmet. A leftover from Green Giant. *Raphael*. Raphael returns to me without certainty, but as I repeat this name a few times I discover a timbre—shaped by a lonely piano and a sorrow-filled cello—that does justice to his face.

The man I remember the most I'll name Juan. Ever since I discovered things can be beautiful because of the care I take to see them, Juan's handsomeness has supported my search for elegance and perfection, even if rough and touched by working hands. Juan's skin is a rich copper color, and in the right sunlight his skin glows and tints his hair with red and gold, his hair always swept back with pomade and combed smooth and glossy and perfect. In his middle years he must've begun to develop a beer belly. No sooner, though, since his T-shirt reveals a chest and biceps defined by muscles as well as a particular youthfulness that would continue on until he died (and in my memory that youthfulness lives beyond his sad death).

He was quiet, like me. Perhaps he was shy like me. He looked at things a long time, all the while making valuable discriminations (something I'm still learning). When he worked he wore a yellow baseball cap, the bill turned down and curved, the shape a pitcher needs when standing on the mound on a bright sunny day. I'll always remember watching him as he leaned against the doorway of a migrant shack, the sun brilliant against arms folded across his chest. I have brief memories of baseball when I was eleven—a few practices, a game, a yellow baseball hat, and a man standing inside the open door of his cream-colored truck watching me as I worked on throwing low strikes. Juan gave me a hand when I fell behind picking corn or bagging potatoes. Later, after I forgot Juan without intending to, I heard he committed suicide by shooting himself in the stomach with a rifle. Something about his quietness stays with me.

Now, as I look out on the bare trees of late November—Thanksgiving has passed, the sun becomes weaker and weaker as the fall ends and winter begins—I see that something seemed continually etched on Juan's brow, appeared to be at work in his memory. What was Juan doing, given the life he seemed to have created in town, out there in those fields? Why did he want or need to work out there? Something must have been at stake for him—*but what?* And when did he reach the point where he felt he had nothing else to gamble?

There were years when I drove past the old Green Giant cannery almost every day, or at least once a week. Sometimes I would pull over, get out of my truck, and look at the crumbling buildings, the sagging roofs, the cement walls seeming soft to the touch, grass and weeds growing up through the cracks, many of the fences surrounding the property rusty and weak, some fallen on their sides. I have no choice but to acknowledge the fact that my mother and father met only because my father traveled from the East Coast in response to a call for workers needed at the cannery. This call is more than likely the only reason Puerto Rican men ever lived in Niles. But I won't accept the possibility that the closing of the cannery and the loss of a job pushed Juan toward death. I have to imagine another side: when the presence of the Green Giant cannery no longer exists, when it seems wiped away from Niles's memory, I'll still return to a region of lost names, a region where I can work to remember how those men lived with dignity. I need the chance to stop on the side of the road in southwestern lower Michigan, look out on the orchards and fields, and demand from the sky and the sun and the earth something like memory and hope and justice . . . even if I can never fully redeem Juan's life.

I'll need to move backward and forward, I'll need to invent the past within the present, the present within the past, if I'm ever to come to terms with this memory. I recognize now that Juan's life is part of a larger pattern crisscrossed by departures, migrations, and arrivals. A larger pattern crisscrossed by sons and daughters within the silence and solitude their fathers leave behind when they depart. A pattern sometimes shaped by violence and death. In my extended family I have relatives who never had a life with their fathers. I often forget that my cousin is part Puerto Rican because her father, a contemporary of my father's, has been lost from memory and, it seems, deliberately forgotten. Her mother, my mother's sister, was briefly married to this man, who migrated to Michigan to work at Green Giant like my father. They had a daughter, my cousin, born three months before I was, and then they split up. I often heard him evoked in a whisper, or in a voice filled with bitter rage. I have the image of a man with longer black hair, brown skin, and a long Pancho Villa mustache—but the image is vague, and it fades away.

I'm not sure I ever actually encountered him as a child, and perhaps my cousin did not either. I do distinctly remember my father—his eyes wide, his hands shaking—saying he had learned that my cousin's father was killed in a bar in Puerto Rico. My father's right hand was clenched into a fist, and then his arm extended, his thumb rising, becoming a knife, as he jammed his hand violently into some imaginary space about waist high.

This man, whom I continue to evoke without a name, I place alongside Juan, adding him permanently to the pattern. Yet what he adds is too sharp; it cuts away whatever meaning I try to create with words. As if the words too must depart when they are exhausted, when they become lost fathers *tired of putting up with certain conditions* (as Ernest J. Gaines writes in *Mozart and Leadbelly: Stories and Essays*).

I see now that when I wrote earlier of memory and hope and justice, I meant that there must be hope if the bloodline—of fathers, language, memory, and generations—is to continue, that I have to work to continue the bloodline, even though I must face the hard reality that I may fail to provide what's needed to help someone carry the bloodline into the future. We each make our own wagers in this life, and I have to see that my gamble—through a life of writing—can be placed alongside those men I worked with. I can continue work in a way that honors the struggle and dignity of their lives, no matter how much of their lives I'll never know. I have to try to bring them—the words, too—*back home.*

And, of course, there's so much for me to still discover. I realize in this writing that I continue to evoke "my father," and yet the truth is that the man I'm evoking I knew only as "Chago."

And the man who died of a knife wound in a bar? I realize for the first time, through this writing, that he is my uncle by marriage. Or should I write, in memory, that he's my uncle by blood?

*
**

My work alongside those men didn't last very long. We may have worked four weeks together. Perhaps only three. We made some good money, but that money helped my father to return to drink. I wanted to be on the football team, practice would begin soon, and then the new school year. Our time together fell apart. When I left the fields my father started riding to work with his friends. There wasn't that much work left at Vollman's Market. There was no more late sweet corn to pick; whatever remained in those unpicked fields was left to dry and wilt in the sun and was plowed back into the soil. There were no more potatoes to bag; a semi-trailer had left the market full of neatly stacked pallets of ten-pound bags, and the pole barn, too, still housed potatoes we had picked and bagged. My father started to drink *con fiebre* (as he liked to say in Spanish of the things he found most exciting) and went into his last time—a year—of being drunk before he began the long sober dream and plan to depart back to Puerto Rico.

Those days of dew, sun, corn, and potatoes will always be a part of me. They are a part of the bloodline I'll work to continue until I die, and then maybe they'll fall apart like crumbled dirt and turn to dust and become a part of the sun and the sky and the earth. They grow in every new word I write. "A new word is like a fresh seed sewn on the ground of the discussion" (Wittgenstein remarks). Or: They grow in each new word that's *sown in earth*.

Although I don't remember the work that much anymore, I nevertheless continue to return to those white shacks, clean and strong amid those rich brown fields, to the thick, tall swaying green trees and the miles of potato fields that went on and on and on. Like blank pieces of paper those shacks wait for my return, they wait for my words.

*
**

My father and his friends shared stories and memories I'm grateful to have been a part of. Their loud laughter and broad smiles are so important, as is their happiness in each other's company. They helped me to know whenever I ate my lunch with them or whenever they called me from my colored sleep inside that shack that there could be much more difficult things in life than working together on a hot summer day.

When I look back, I'm haunted by seasons—those seasons of fruits and vegetables, cold and heat, abundance and decay. My looking back has never been simply to emphasize a season of change, nor to compare my living beyond change. My looking back is more of a deep recognition of how a season leaves and we then suddenly return to who we are, a temporary vessel of ragged skins and brittle bones bearing the loss of what has just departed. Yesterday the sun was topaz and warm in the leaves, and the sun stayed with the twilight for some time as I started to count the emerging stars. Today the clouds hang heavy and wet in a bunched-together sky, the last of the leaves falling to the ground when the northwest wind shakes the trees. Yesterday a man walked at my side down a farm lane, one of his arms tucked under my arm in support, the other helping me to hold up a wet burlap sack brimming with ears of corn. Today he helps me again as I write these words, compose one sentence after another, each like a furrow in a field sown with seeds—seeds of anticipation, seeds of patience, seeds unafraid of the days that must pass before the harvest.

Blue Memory

As big as a loaf of bread, or maybe a pineapple or yucca root, cradled in his arm, I'm swaddled in a white blanket patterned with little ducks, eyes closed, my memory still awash in the sea of birth. My father holds me close to his chest. He's wearing the most beautiful blue shirt; it's clean, pressed, bright, the material soft and shiny, silky, the sleeves and shoulders generously cut. He smiles, his face full of color, his hair swept back with pomade. He's sitting on a couch, holds me in the curve of his arms, in his wide, strong hands, thick veins running along his tendons, over his knuckles. He no longer works at Green Giant picking mushrooms in the dark growing houses: I was born in Three Rivers, down the road in another town, so now he stands on an assembly line for General Motors. I'm light, wrapped in the blanket, my two little brown fists, my pink face, and a crown of thick, dark hair. A soft, brief pause from the pulsating machines, the roar of air and steel all around him crashing against the concrete floor, booming through his body. My father's hands leave an impression I sometimes still feel across my shoulders, along the back of my head. No longer in the photo, here in this writing, for the first time, my father teaches me the memory of blue.

Part III
ISLAND

. . . he was hoping the picture would bring the whole thing back.

—SAM SHEPARD, MOTEL CHRONICLES

Up Jumped Spring

The birds loud in the lilacs. Inside the hospital room I sip a pink concoction through a straw. It's chalky, the bitter taste of aspirin breaking on my tongue, a bit of cough syrup and bad milk that crawls down into my stomach. The medicine will show up like bright tracings everywhere it touches. I lie back on the gurney. The sun yellows the windows, and on the wall I watch the outline of the lilacs and the shadows of birds springing from them in small smudges. The nurse wheels me down the hall, through the opened double doors, and I'm lifted onto a new gurney under a machine that will discover the flow of pink within my body. There will now be more bills. My mother missing work even though she scheduled the earliest appointment possible. My mother losing pay she can never make back. There is more shame because the doctor finally says he cannot find anything wrong. This last test doesn't reveal anything, why some days I eat nothing, why some days I eat too much, why I become so nauseated, my stomach full of nervous pain, sometimes breaking down into uncontrollable weeping. Sometimes sitting on the edge of my bed and punching myself in the stomach.

Maybe I made it all up. Maybe, the doctor recommended, a visit to a therapist. Maybe I could see Dr. Dale, who overprescribed painkillers, antidepressants, and antianxiety meds to anyone who asked. The same doctor who helped commit my grandmother to the Kalamazoo Regional Psychiatric Hospital. *You better straighten up or they'll take you up to Kalamazoo.* My grandmother who walked in circles too. In the evening, with all the lights off, she sat moaning in a chair, rocking back and forth, her arms across her stomach, crying out that she was just too nervous.

Maybe it was too much for my parents to openly talk about alcoholism and an emotionally unstable son. And maybe, in the end, it was easiest to decide there was nothing wrong with me. I never tried to swallow a whole bottle of pills. Maybe I was just a young boy, like most boys, confused by wanting to love his father while learning to hate him. Confused by the words he couldn't say. A boy adrift in the sensations of memory: of a handsome, strong, hardworking father who held him in his arms, took him to the beach, the sea, blue rising waves, fishing. Who bought him a regal red rooster, black-and-white rabbits, and his first dog, a brown shorthaired pointer. A father, on Saturday, making a red kite. A father who shared with him a faraway paradise. The screaming, the rage in his face, an overturned table, a suitcase thrown into the backseat, the door slammed shut. The rum bottle in a paper bag tucked under the back porch inside the empty square of a concrete block. His hard knuckles striking the top of my skull. His trembling hands. His silence. The long afternoons passed out on the couch, out in the snow, underneath a tree.

*
**

"You do not stop hungering for your father's love, even after you are grown up," Paul Auster writes in *The Invention of Solitude.* Later my mother confessed, *I had been afraid because you seemed so depressed, spent so much time alone in your room. I was always scared you might take down your shotgun.*

★
★★

Today is April 26, spring is green in the fields and trees, the crab apple and dogwoods are in full bloom, and at first light I sit with a steaming cup of black coffee and the loud birds. I hear Pablo Neruda, "Why does spring once again / offer its green clothes?" April 26: my father's birthday. A spring long ago my father brought home a brown dog. His tail had been clipped, he walked with his head down, and we called him Eeyore. (Was it my father who came up with that name?) Everywhere I walked, Eeyore followed, he ran with me through the fields and along the beach, and when I sat against a gravestone, I would rub the soft brown hair on the top of his head, his chin resting on my thigh, the dogwood blossoms dropping coins of shade and light on my arms and hands, Eeyore's brown eyes.

¿Por qué otra vez la primavera / ofrece sus vestidos verdes?
Why would you want to forget all that's green, Papi?

★
★★

My mother and I laughed in the car as we left the hospital. Maybe all we needed was for someone to tell us nothing was wrong, it would all be okay with the passing of time. No more expensive tests. The trees along the road bloomed with pink and white flowers. The river was high and glinted with gold currents. Over the weekend my mother had picked up a shirt and a pair of shoes at a garage sale. The shoes looked like they were for soccer—white with black stripes and thin rubber soles. Almost brand new. The brown shirt was collared, a polo shirt, sporty with orange stripes across the chest and along the shoulders. They were someone else's clothes, sure, but for now they were mine until I outgrew them, and then maybe someone else would wear them. If anyone asked about them at school, I'd smile and fain indifference. Tell them my father had brought them from Puerto Rico. They are part of the new style (and in solitude, I'd say, *part of the new boy I must become*). My father would soon return home, though it must have always been hard when he had to leave his island, where, every morning, through a blue mosquito net, he would watch the swaying palms outside his window and then follow their shadows move along the gray concrete wall like hands, waving hands, hands calling him to rise: *Chago, come outside, come out and walk the red road, taste these golden mangoes, follow the hummingbirds over the green mountains.*

Ox in the Dusk

I was out in the cane field crying. Pink bands of light striped the sky and outlined the edges of the green mountains, and all around me the bats rose and dipped and swerved in the fading light. I stepped toward the ox. The field deepened like a bruise in the dusk. The black and gray spots that peppered the ox's hide blurred—his legs kicking up dust, his chain rattling, a bent piece of steel anchoring the silver links into the dirt. My father had left without me, had walked down the red road, bent below a row of mango trees, and disappeared into the jungle. I was trying to find something to stare at to stop my tears: a funnel of bats swerving out of the mountains, some stalks of cane stirring in the sea breeze, a banana tree swaying, the dust caked on the ox's hooves. There was a party in a different barrio. My father, elegant in a parade of music, food, and drink, swirling from one conversation to another. He had wanted to take me, but my grandmother, my Abuela, had said, *No, no sir, no senōr, Freddie is not going*. I wiped my nose with my forearm and stepped closer to the ox. His head turned toward me, the chain rising up straight and hard against his shoulder. Daylight was quickly running through the dusk into night. The muscles on his shoulder, under his hide, rippled. His wet eyes looked tired and sore, flies circling in front of them.

My father and I had traveled together to his childhood island for a two-week visit. I remember I was nine years old. One night he had taken me to a festival. The plaza was crowded with people and colorful lights for el Dia de los Tres Reyes. I had been to Puerto Rico before at the age of two, and as we walked in the plaza many faces looked familiar, each smell—roasting pork, wet banana leaves, dry hay, freshly cut coconut—was pleasant and comforting, my body beginning to sway to music I must have tried to dance to before I could even utter a sentence. The food stalls and amusement rides sparkled with light, and in the middle a fountain shot up small drops of water sparkling like fireflies. On a table, under a canopy of canvas, masks with long, pointed horns and noses grimaced in yellow, black, and red. There were machetes made of wood and painted maracas from dried gourds. In a miniature country house there was a table with tiny pots, spoons, forks, knives, and cups arranged on top. Hanging from the rafters was a long bundle of green bananas, a mesh bag filled with oranges, and a freshly plucked chicken, its eyes like shiny bits of glass, the rope around its still feathered neck streaked with blood. At the next stall heat lamps cast down their strong light on candied apples and pink cotton candy spinning like clouds, and white paper boats held saffron-tinted *bacalatoís*, their crispy edges like delicate lace. I turned and my father was gone. He had already been walking unevenly, more sideways than straight, slurring his words, his eyes closing between steps. I walked and walked past the stalls, up and down the aisles, looked hard at the faces I passed, and circled around the fountain, only to discover I was lost.

An older couple asked for my Abuela. They each took a hand and led me through the plaza. A long line of cars snaked down the road before the turn to Abuela's barrio—and there in the passing headlights Abuela paced, her hands behind her back, looking at the approaching cars. She was waiting as if she knew something was wrong. I write these fleeting memories and continue to experience loss, wonder once again what I hope to accomplish besides feeling inadequate, small, trivial. I never had a chance to ask her about that memory, how it was that she knew to walk to the end of the road and wait. What vision did she possess? Had that couple called? Was it possible that my father got scared, gave up searching for me, and then found his way back home? Before I realized I needed to ask her, Abuela died. My stomach clenches, then releases something like water or blood or inner light, a wave of butterflies rising inside my chest. Images, smells, the taste of cilantro, the wet thud of breadfruit falling to the ground, an intuition to sit still. Wait. Just stay here without expectation. Let the butterflies gather. I see the white ox: he lifts his leg, his shoulder ripples, and he shakes his head, his tail whipping in the air. I move closer. The chain clinks. The bats swerve across the sky, the thick green of the mountains feeling close enough to touch, and the day runs faster toward night, the cane stalks a stark bone white, their tops tinted purple. In the dusk I touch his side, feel his hard shoulder. Hear Abuela calling for me to come back home.

I was most often alone during the day. Sometimes I'd find a group of local boys for an impromptu baseball game in Abuela's big patio or out on the red dirt road. Mostly I chased lizards, ran between the house's cool shadows and the warm sun, or followed the cane field to its end, where a mountain stream flowed to the sea, shrimp and crabs darting in its clear currents. And looking up at the mountains, I caught the speck of a red or white shirt as someone slowly made his way to the top. I dreamt of the day when I might follow the same path and make my way down to the other side.

***

One night Abuela took me down the road to the end of the barrio and then followed another road to a big yellow house. Abuela and I are sitting in the living room when a young woman comes home from work. She's wearing a cream-colored silk shirt and dark slacks. Her hair is cut in a bob just below her ears, feathered down the middle, straight and deep brown, as are her eyes, her eyelashes thick and long. She is much whiter than Abuela, her skin smooth like her shirt. She speaks English well and asks all kinds of questions about my visit, my school, and what I like to do back home. Who is this second or third cousin? Colored memory: the gleaming blue-and-yellow Spanish tiles, the lime green couch, the white walls, and out the open window, less than an arm's length away, dark green leaves brightened by oranges. We sit in the living room watching *Bonnie & Clyde* on the small black-and-white television and eat one orange after another. When I wake up she is lying next to me, turned away toward the window now filling with sunlight. I look up into the white mosquito nets swaying overhead, face the cool morning air turning from a black fan, and pull the soft sheet closer. She turns over, looks into my eyes. I will remember her face forever, though I cannot recollect her name. When I return to that house, hold her face in my eyes, I'm often standing in the bedroom doorway. I see the double bed high off the floor, the small steps—three—needed to get up on the bed, the four posts of carved wood, and the fluttering mosquito nets. Like a cocoon, like a thin mist, like skin I'll never feel again. Her face, those eyes, the way her bangs fluttered in the breeze from the fan's turning. She continues to appear in my dreams. The nets forever swaying to a music only I can hear. The scent of oranges still on my hands.

*
**

Never around for breakfast or dinner, the mosquito net over my father's bed never stirring. One day I saw his blue shirt up on the roof, his shoulders darkened with streaks of sweat, as he carried pieces of rebar or swung concrete blocks into place and helped his father build an addition to the house. Blue memory: the orange-and-purple flame of a propane torch lying on the ground, my index finger passing through, and the pain hotter than the sun on my face as I clutched my hand under my arm. When I looked up, the deep azure sky, a few puffy clouds drifting by. As if someone had snuffed out his shirt. My father gone.

One night Abuela took me to a *parranda*. We walked a thin path through some trees and stood on a dirt road in the dusk. At the end of the road was a row of houses that faced the mountains, their white and yellow and lime paint faded and peeling. Lamp and candlelight glowed in their front yards. A group of men carried a palanquin on the road, a gold nativity scene on top encircled by votive candles, blue- and red- and green-robed figures gathered around Jesus. Camels and lambs looked on, piles of hay and buckets on the ground, an open chest glinting with shiny gifts. Mary and Joseph knelt in front of Jesus, their faces and hands stilled in prayer. Bats swarmed in the last bit of pink sky. The thrum of a cuatro guitar took to the air, followed by the scratch of a guiro, and then softly shaken maracas. Abuela led me inside and fixed me a plate of chicken and rice with a *pastale*. The young woman stood against the sink. She came forward, touched my shoulder, and pulled me close. My face warmed. *Have you climbed your mountain yet? When will you sleep over again?*

People stood in a semicircle whispering. Underneath a mango tree lay a man, facedown, without shirt or shoes. His skin—his bare feet, his naked back—blazed in the lamplight. Abuela stepped close, called out my father's name—*Chaging, Chaging, Chaging*. She shook his shoulder. Her voice held a bit of grief when she asked, *Chago?* He had black hair, his bare shoulders as familiar as my reflection in the mirror. My mouth went dry, my throat tight, my heart hot in my chest as Abuela continued to shake him. Slowly his shoulders hunched up, he raised to his elbows and knees, his broad back turning, his hair and face askew, his eyes shiny and wild. He focused on Abuela. He sprang to his feet, swayed under the tree just as Abuela jumped back. She grabbed her wrist and pressed her palm against her chest as if his shoulder had burned her fingers. The crowd broke out in laughter. I laughed too. He stumbled, his arms swaying at his sides, then his hands rising to reach the shadows of the tree. He walked to them, crookedly, out into the night beyond the lamplight.

Sons of working-class alcoholics live thin, vulnerable lives. You strive to work hard, keep busy, your shoulder heavy against the grindstone. Walk a straight line, stop at all the stop signs, never run a red light. A few beers, a pint of whiskey, a bottle of wine help because you deserve a break from work, from remembering. Your body, nevertheless, should never rest—always in motion and ready to work, walk the street or drive down the road. Never give your heart the chance to give up. Never rest or it will fill with regret. My memory never stops, like a wagon wheel churning on a steep muddy road. I continue to see the mango tree and the man lying facedown. One day, many years later, I tried to create the image in words. I had read a handful of books in my life, had never wanted to write a thing, and yet there I was. It was raining. I had opened a cheap notebook, listened to the rain like small pieces of glass pattering the roof of my attic apartment, and some mysterious energy welled up within me until I shattered with desire. I wrote without knowing what I was doing, where I might go, where the words might take me.

I remember the smell of the rain against the rusty screen, see my younger self bent over a red card table writing in a notebook—or was it the notebook and the pen that pulled me to the table, closer to the letters, the notebook and pen and table and letters writing me, sowing within me this memory that never stops growing?

What was it that drove me to bring together the broken pieces, to meld together the details of this personal mythology? It was there in every hard-pressed letter on the page. *A. O. X. C H A G O.* My memory grew of Abuela and that young boy who had gone days without seeing his father, wondering where he was, why he had disappeared. That father who had taken him to visit a colorful island, a forever paradise. *Santiago.* That father. A secret wish: night, the glow of lamplight, a mango tree, and as we eat its golden fruit our memories taste sweet and everlasting.

I loved to cross the dirt road, swing my leg through the barbwire fence, duck below the top wire, and step into the cane field with a long knife. I stopped in the middle of a row, chose a stalk, and quickly sliced through. Carefully, I peeled away the hard green-and-brown skin until I arrived at the wet, white fruit. Sucked the juice until only the stringy fiber was left. The sensation cool and sweet, like nothing I had ever tasted before, and I thought that if I were ever stranded on an island, the first thing I'd do is find a cane field. My mind went blank with the taste of the juice, the feel of the cool stream running down my chin and along the back of my hand as I walked to the row's end, descended, and then walked up a small hill where the dirt was clear of cane, tamped down smooth and hard, red as fresh blood even in the dusk.

*
**

I am still alone in that room. I can't appease or stop the pain in my stomach and a deep pocket of nausea pulls it down into my back and thighs and when I walk it feels as if something is shaking and trembling from inside and at any given moment I may stumble and fall—or simply shatter. I am afraid, worried, ashamed about what might happen. I lose a piece of my life, so deep inside my nausea it's as if I'm possessed. The house is empty. I walk back and forth from the kitchen to the living room, create a circle in front of the brown couch and the console with the eight-track player and TV, and then take to the stairs—up and down, up and down, up and down. My arms across my stomach, tears forming, and a thin path worn into the thick carpet. Every creaking step ingrained in the soles of my feet. It's always the same: afternoon, after school, nothing to do, the light muted, and I wonder when my father will come home, whether he'll be happy or angry, sober or drunk. And whenever he's home it's like being around a person going mad—full of rage, in constant motion: leaves to rake, a fence to paint, a garden to weed, a car that needs repair, a goat or rabbit to cut up and cook.

Was he angry because I wasn't working? Every time he looked at me did he remember his childhood of work? Was he struggling with a grief he had no words for? Was he trying to tell me that I was not like him, or that I must run as far away from him as I can?

I can't leave the room. I have to wait for that other father, imagine him on the other side of memory: nothing. I wait. No one. Then my hands clench into fists. I sit down in a chair. Raise my fists high, and then it begins: one punch after another—thigh, stomach, thigh—after another. Just before sleep, in front of a mirror, naked, I look for the green-and-yellow circles, the odd-shaped clouds, lakes, and islands on my thighs and stomach. There's one along my ribs like a blooming rose. I strike it a few more times, feel the warmth spread across my stomach, the sharp tingling like a knife rising from inside to stab my skin. I get dressed. Won't look at it again because I know sometime in the night it will change, transform in size and shape to become something more than memory. Almost blue, always true. *Plus plus plus.*

An old, crooked man stopped on the road. His straw hat was tipped back, revealing his sun-wrinkled eyes and toothy smile. His work-worn hands: one held the barbed wire fence, the other a machete. *Toro, toro, toro. Be careful, caballero, or the bull will get you.* Maybe there was danger if I stepped too close, but the old man's voice sounded so excited and happy, full of daring: *Go, step closer, go run your hand along his shoulder, his nose, those sharp horns.*

Standing in the ox's shadow. Crying. Stepping closer and listening to his wet breath, the clink of his chain, saliva dripping from his tongue. We stood there watching the daylight run away, the cane field and mountains meeting the night as the bats rose around us and their erratic flight drew the waves that pushed us closer. The cane leaves stirred, parted, and a boy stood there. He said, his face shiny with sweat, *Don't cry, don't cry, your papa will come back.*

Ají Dulce

A stallion and three mares trotted in a field of red dirt. Clumps of
tall grasses grew along the field's edges. The stallion began galloping back and forth across the field, dust rising in clouds over his
legs, and with each turn back he circled the mares into a tighter
group. His eyes were black frantic pools, and his long mane shook
every time he nickered and nudged the mares' necks and backs. He
slowed next to a dark brown mare, nibbled her neck, and grabbed
her mane with his teeth and pulled her away from the others. Their
bodies were lean and muscular, their coats smooth and shiny. The
stallion reared up, whinnied, and when his front hooves touched
the ground he pawed the dirt. His nose nudged the mare's rump
several times, and the black wrinkly sack between his legs started
to stretch, grew and grew in size, and to my young boy's eyes the
stallion's penis grew at least two feet, hard and sharp below his
stomach and pointed toward the red dirt. His eyes widened even
more, and he mounted the mare and bit down on her neck as she
slowly stretched it and dropped her nose, her eyes just as wide and
dark and frantic as the stallion's.

Wepa . . . Dale . . . Asi, chico, asi . . . rose in a loud chorus from the edge of the field, followed by hearty laughter. A group of men were sitting underneath a grove of flamboyant trees. Some wore white hard hats—telephone company workers raising new poles and connecting lines—the other men were dressed in nice pants and guayaberas. They all sat on small stools and crates eating from paper plates, the ground sparking with the flaming blossoms that dropped from the trees, as they watched the horses in the field.

See how they play? my father asked. He giggled, his cheeks red. I felt blood rise to the edge of my ears. I tried to smile back but my jaw trembled. The stallion whinnied again and rocked against the mare's rump. *Asi, chico . . .* And the laughter rose again.

My father walked down the road. We were waiting for a *carro publico.* When I turned back, all four horses were bunched together nibbling on the long grass, the barbwire fence fracturing their figures into cubed fragments and impressions, as if they shared the same legs or necks. And such a mix of red as I'd never seen before— the red dirt, the reddish-brown horses, the brassy gold glinting in the stallion's mane mixing with the tawny brown of the mares'. Their eyes shining with dust. The wind picked up, the crimson blossoms on the shaking flamboyants drifting in the air, and I noticed for the first time the long stalks of sugar cane and the mountains looking down in dark green.

I often find myself walking in a field surrounded by swaying trees. There'll be the scent of eucalyptus or pine. A hawk in the high blue sky drifting on invisible currents. The strong smell of hot dust or manure, perhaps the aroma of the sea. Even if the field is empty I see horses running, red dust powdering their hooves and legs, the wind stirring the hair on their outstretched necks.

The fall to the soil of a plump mango from a heavy afternoon rain, the birth of a clear azure sky broken by torn, puffy clouds, the sun sparkling on the red dirt road, and then a young boy with no shirt, his skin a little darker

than the dirt, his jeans streaked with dust all the way down to his bare feet,
and when he pulls the hemp bridle he and a sorrel horse gently trot by, the
boy's hair slick and still, the horse's neck taut, its blond mane fluttering with
el brisa de la mar.

I write these words, step back into that January afternoon, and
song gallops across the fields of memory:

> *That night in January*
> *who did you go see,*
> *like a colt chomping at his bit?*

And my desire bites through, and, with blood in my mouth, I spit
it out into the dust.

*
**

When we finally made it up the mountain that I dreamed day after
day of crossing, it was as if nothing happened. My father and the
men followed a thin, red path that darkened with shadows from the
overarching trees and bamboo. The air cooled as if we were walking
toward ice. They stopped. Looked. We stood in front of the mountain, and falling from its slope was a silver stream that gathered into
a pool bounded by black boulders, green and yellow leaves floating
on its surface like boats seen from a great distance. My father broke
off a wide leaf from a wild banana tree and crossed from boulder
to boulder and stuck it into the mountain's face, water tumbling
in a silver-and-white curtain into the pool, the bamboo leaning in.

The shade was cold, the mountain blocking half the sky and
the jungle seeming to swallow the other half. Up through the treetops jagged holes through the thick leaves revealed the sky. The
men—my father, my uncle Ismael, and a distant cousin—undressed.
They waded into the pool, plunged down holding their noses, slowly

fell forward and under. Water splashing and raining from the men, the tumbling stream. Someone had brought a bar of soap. My father lathered up, stood on a boulder underneath the banana leaf he had placed in the stream, and let the water shower on his body until it was clear and his skin gleamed. The men laughed, splashed each other, dove into the pool, rose, white foamy circles forming underneath the stream tumbling into the pool. These were men who had worked hard from a young age, and they were lean and graceful and smooth, arms roped with muscles, stomachs firm, and they held their brown bodies straight and tall. My uncle soaped his thighs, scrubbed his stomach, his hands quickly rising and rubbing under his arms. My father was the whitest, and though his arms and legs and chest were brown, his buttocks and the tops of his thighs were like snow. He called me in.

I was fat, too conscious of what I might look like naked, and so I undressed slowly. Without taking my underwear off, I stepped in, the water colder and clearer than any I had ever encountered. I went under. I saw the men's legs flash by, tiny pink shrimp schooling together and lit by the weak, cloudy light falling through, and on the surface of the pool the undersides of the small boatlike leaves that floated on silver-green waves. When I came up Ismael was singing a sad and beautiful bolero, his clear voice finding the spaces in between the silence and the tumbling stream. Just like the men I soaped up my body, stood underneath the stream, and left my eyes open so I could see them through all the falling water. This was the mountain I had wanted more than anything to cross. Here it was crossing me, bathing me, and that had to be enough. There was nothing else to ask for or remember. I cupped the pool in my hands, clouds and silver sky reflected within, and tasted for the first time *agua dulce*. My father and his brother stood side by side, up to their knees in the pool, their shoulders touching, white next to dark brown. Their black mustaches glistened with drops of water, their smiles, the red in their cheeks and their clear bright eyes—there was a love between them I didn't know. It is only now, morning after morning, when I listen to the water falling behind them, look closely at their young faces, that I begin to discover words that take me between shadow and dream, take me to a pool of life where I can touch them just as surely as my hand touches my stomach, warm, hard, wet with yesterday.

*
**

As I'm writing these words I look at a photograph I took of my uncle Ismael. Such an elegant moment, even in all its broken and cobbled-together simplicity. Ismael's slacks, his open-collared shirt, the drape of his arm, and the cigarette in his hand. The faint ridge of a vein running along the inside of his arm. His smile. There's only a fragmented, poor life here—broken concrete blocks, scraps of wood, twigs and leaves, a jagged piece of corrugated tin. But just on the other side of the road, where Ismael is gazing, I can find all of them as a part of my Abuela's and abuelo's house. And even in the silence of this photograph I hear his song.

All the men in my father's family are handsome, and anyone can clearly see this in my uncle's face: his dark eyes happy with rum and his cooking, his smile, and the perfection of his arms and hands, the pointed cigarette, the silver spoon. *Ismael.* He's cooking a goat or chicken stew with big chunks of yucca and *ñame* and potatoes and a sauce from lard colored by achiote seeds that browns the pieces of meat a rich saffron. There's garlic, onion, cilantro, oregano, and several green, yellow, and orange *ají dulce* peppers. He stirs in a small can of *salsa de tomate.* There's the sharp sound of the silver spoon striking the lip of the aluminum pot so all the pieces, juices, and flavors fall back inside, and there's the scrape of the spoon along the bottom so nothing burns over the wood fire. We eat the steaming stew in bowls with white rice. It is a windy day. Even though the photo is in black and white, I see there's an overcast sky, and Ismael has the piece of tin propped up with a board next to the fire to block the wind. I don't remember if he cooked the stew before or after our swim. There, under the mango tree, I shiver and let the smoke and the fire, the smell and the flavors, run warmly along my arms. That's what I remember. *Ismael*, I call, raise my silver-and-black camera, and press the button over my eye.

Patio Dreams

Piragua

When I was strong enough Abuela let me lift the tin pail from underneath the kitchen sink and carry it out to her patio, where I swung the pail back and then flung the water up into the air. Every Friday she gave me twenty-five cents, and on Saturday mornings we followed a thin snaking path over the mountain. Once in town, she made her way down a blue stone road shaded by lime and yellow houses, her shopping bag in the crook of her arm, and I sat in the plaza on a bench with a *piragua de coco*. I still remember the man's black arm against his white guayabera, the bulge of his biceps as his arm moved up and down quickly, his hand digging into the giant block of ice, the shavings like snowflakes falling on his arms, jumping between us, catching on my forehead, my lips, on the ends of my eyelashes. Cold. Warm. Sitting on the bench, the sun on my face, coconut ice swimming in the deep pocket of my stomach.

Back at the patio, in the early-morning light, the air still cool from the sea and redolent of salt and almonds, I stand in front of the chicken coop. I rear back and fling the water in the tin pail as far as I can, imagine I have the power to throw waves and turn the patio into a rolling sea as I listen for the hard snap of water against the ground, the red earth shining with silver and purple soap bubbles, and the chickens scatter like white sails cutting through waves as they peck pieces of onion, kernels of rice, orange rinds, and mango skins, the drowned blossoms and stems of cilantro floating like seaweed. The dirt smells clean. The sea's alive with bobbing chickens. The waves I had thrown roll one after the other across my Abuela's patio, gather at my feet, lift me up, and carry me back into her house.

Tree Within

Up every morning with the sun to make coffee, Abuela cooks three meals a day and keeps her house spotless. You could eat off her floors. Every two weeks she propped a ladder against the house, checked the cistern, and cleaned the troughs of leaves so the water that collected there and ran down to her kitchen was clear and clean and blue. She would often hum a song as she worked. She was eighty-nine, of course of a different age, and even if her life seemed simple it possessed more dignity than many will ever encounter. One morning she said her stomach hurt, and after being admitted to the hospital she seemed to feel better. Soon she was coughing up spots of blood that gradually turned into a rushing stream, her last breaths coloring a towel.

Her cabinets were rose pink, as were the hard tiles that covered the floor. She said that when the sun warmed the kitchen in the early morning, she felt the red dirt patio like blood running into her house (*el mar de sangre*). The water from her roof was always cool, redolent of oranges and mangos. The kitchen and patio were one: the back door forever open, no glass in the windows, only the hand-cranked aluminum blinds, the green-headed hummingbirds hovering over the table ready to dip into the silver pitcher and taste Abuela's sweet water. After she died the oldest orange tree stopped bearing fruit. Its limbs and bark turned black. Her dented pots still hung over the sink, as well as her pink coffee mugs, and on the counter the small cast iron skillet she cooked her eggs in, their bright yellow suns looking up and bubbling in a circle of hot black.

Ten years after her death and her kitchen was still the same. The floors duller, a few tiles cracked; the smell of dust drew me to the window, where I saw the orange tree had fallen across the patio. That night in Abuela's bedroom, the blue mosquito nets swayed me to sleep and I dreamed of a room lit by a black light on one side and a pink light on the other, a mild breeze causing the orange tree's limbs to gently tap the roof. On the wall of the room there was a photograph of Abuela's large family, some twenty girls in white ruffled dresses, the lights shadowing the image. I couldn't recognize a young Abuela. On a shelf there was a jar with a lead lid, and inside a miniature white house. Next to Abuela's favorite knife and her worn cutting board (its grain shiny with fruit oils) lay her death mask cast in pink plaster. Looking closer, someone had run a knife down its center—from forehead through nose down to her chin—and removed the mask's flesh, revealing the plaster underneath, pristine as a fresh bandage.

Once, she cut a tender green branch from her orange tree, shaved down the end until the wood's flesh appeared like a clean bone, and placed it in a tin cup, the tips of her brown fingers glistening with the clean water from her sink. Weeks later we stood side by side, her arm around my shoulder, my head against her chest, and watched as a few blossoms began to bloom.

Out of This World

Gaston Bachelard writes, "Memories of the outside world will never have the same tonality as those of home and, by recalling these memories, we add to our store of dreams; we are never real historians, but always near poets, and our emotion is perhaps nothing but an expression of a poetry that was lost" (*The Poetics of Space*). Standing in front of María Brito's *El Patio de Mi Casa*, my two worlds blended or bled into each other, colors and images breaking through the wall of her evocative kitchen and patio. Inside outside, outside inside. Nightly dreams more vivid, and I awoke with the taste of memory in my mouth. When I ran my tongue against my palate, along my teeth, over my lips, the dreams shuddered within, the strong scent and taste of blood and earth in my nose. Like the meeting of light and shadow, kitchen and patio, night and day, memory and dream became one. María Brito's beautiful art returned to me sensations and objects, fragments and echoes I'd almost lost forever. "The great function of poetry is to give us back our dreams," Bachelard writes. Yes, I must accept this poetry, ecstatically, as I imagine and dream a place out of this world.

Dream of a Dying Tree

In my patio there's a dying tree bursting from the middle of my crib that rises toward the sky, a lone arm pointing like a compass needle magnetized to night. The crib is a ship, and the ship holds the sea, and at the center of the sea like a star is a floating island, and the island is a dying tree. One shipwreck after another has thrown its wreckage into the crib, this ship or raft or island that is a star within a dying tree. Its long trunk rising to the sky like a ship's mast, like a flagpole without a flag standing in my patio marking an island at the center of the sea, glowing like a star burning in the middle of the night through the limbs of a dying tree. Growing from the middle of my crib, a tree, blackened by sea winds and the sharp crack of lightning, pieces of wood splintered from the dying tree that never wanted to be anything other than a tree bursting from the red earth of an island floating in the middle of the sea. *El patio de mi casa, mi casa de mi patio*, the backyard of my house where my crib became a tree, and before the tree was a burning star or a sea of azure waves or a ship with a tall mast creaking in the wind, it had only one name: *Dream of a Tree.*

Calendar

After his mother died, my father saved one object from her kitchen: a small wall calendar from the Ricomini Bakery. It is simple and cheap—thin white paper, each day of the week signified by the miniature black letters on the top, and each single square for a day printed with a bold black number in the upper right corner. *December 1990* in bigger red letters stands centered at the very top of the sheet, where two staples hold it in place, and once a month ends it is easy to tear away the days. Abuela had circled some days, boxed others, and with broad pencil strokes crossed out many. Above the twenty-fourth there is a cursive word—*piragua, papa, patio, panaderia*—I can't make out. When my father gave me the calendar, he didn't express much more than that it was from her kitchen. Why would I want it? Perhaps because I'm a writer, he hoped I might be able to read it, might discover a key to its lines and colors and numbers.

Abuela's calendar: here is a room of her days, a month of her life that I cannot name. I see Abuela in her kitchen, steam rising from a gray pot, the blue-and-yellow pattern of her dress becoming a field of flowers rippling as she hums and sways to some lonely sounding song, the leaves of a banana tree scraping against the wall from the breeze stirring the tree and pushing the leaves through the window. Many memories lay hidden within the steam that rises only to suddenly disappear.

Gaston Bachelard writes, "And if we want to go beyond history, or even, while remaining in history, detach from our own history the always too contingent history of the persons who have encumbered it, we realize that the calendars of our lives can only be established in its imagery."

I am alone with the weight of her days, the silence of her calendar, this history I might save. From the shadows of palms I step back into the kitchen, take a chair in the corner, and sit down. I begin to remember this house, where I learned to dream dreams without any significance greater than the ochre-throated hummingbird hovering over the bowl of yellow-and-green-and-red mangoes ripening on the table next to Abuela's cutting board and her long silver knife glinting in the morning light.

Part IV
OUT OF THIS WORLD

On the bank by the spring creek
my shadow seemed to leap
up to gather me, or it leapt
up to gather me, not seeming so
but as a natural fact.

—JIM HARRISON, "THE THEORY & PRACTICE OF RIVERS"

Grand Marais

Having read enough of Jim Harrison's writings, I imagined that
if I were in the Dunes Saloon at 10:00 p.m. I might find him at a
back table with a glass of whiskey. I was beginning my first semester
at Purdue University, and my life had utterly changed. Just a few
months before, I'd quit the factory, the only steady part of my life
for the last five years. Attending classes had become boring. I was
restless, and I found that, oddly, my body ached for the return of
physical exhaustion. Fall break began and I drove the roughly six
hundred miles to Grand Marais, up on the shores of Lake Superior,
the freshwater sea, to meet Jim Harrison.

The Dunes Saloon was the most crowded bar I'd ever seen. I
sat on a stool drinking one beer after another, along with shots
of whiskey, and every so often, as the hour approached, I glanced
over my left shoulder to see if Harrison entered and sat down. He
never arrived, I became happily drunk, and when I returned to my
campsite I built a fire and looked up at a million stars, bright and
clear with the blue of a frozen lake gathering them all together.
Inside my VW van I pulled an extra wool blanket over my sleeping

bag. My breath was a white cloud that rose toward the van's roof and disappeared. I looked out the side windows and through the treetops to see the stars and the sky press closer.

Earlier that evening I'd written a letter to Harrison. I had a manila envelope stuffed with everything I had written: a handful of short stories, a short novel I composed in four days filled with fishing, drinking, cutting wood, and epilepsy, along with several vignettes, and pages of lyric poetry. The letter shared ruminations too personal, too future-oriented, and it was filled with all kinds of doubt. I tried to express how Harrison's work spoke to me and how thankful I was for his writing. But my letter wasn't as much addressed to him as it was a confession wherein I expressed uncertainty whether or not going to school was a good idea, even if I had already set my sights on a PhD. I thought, in fact, I might write for my dissertation a scholarly biography focused on Harrison's work. All I wanted, though, deep down, was to write. I wrote to Harrison without giving any background or context, almost as if he knew parts of my life, as if we were friends, or at the very least he knew where I was from. It was an immediate, spontaneous act—and yet, I had brought all my writings with me in the manila envelope.

On Sunday I awoke to a pounding head and queasy stomach. It was a cold and sunny day. The blue was bright in the van's windows, and I rolled over and tried to sleep. When I finally got up, I walked to the campground's shower room. I dropped two quarters into the shower's timer, the water falling strong and hot as I scrubbed away and started to feel clean and brand new, the pounding in my head turning to a dull throb. And that was a good thing because I had awoken in the middle of the night as if in a dream, jerked the van's side door open, leapt to the ground, and trotted as far as I could from the campsite because I knew I'd never make it to the bathroom. Under the bright stars I had the worst case of watery runs ever, all those drinks and the juicy cheeseburger I'd eaten moving through me like a stream. Besides a couple of older fishermen camped on the other side of the campground with a trailer and a boat, I was the only one there. Still, I covered my middle-of-the-night runs with sand, dirt, and leaves before heading back to my van and a peaceful sleep.

After my shower I rode my bike around the village's short four blocks and then followed the winding road east along the lake to the graveyard and the dirt lanes through the headstones. I read names and dates, repeated some out loud so they might stay with me. I returned along the road and stopped at a gas station and got a coffee and a plastic-wrapped raspberry Danish. I sat on a bench up on the bluff. The harbor and bay were as smooth as glass. There was a short wall of fog retreating north, white sailboats floating like sleeping swans, their rigs stored, their reflections sharp on the sea's surface. I walked back past the gas station and across the street to the saloon, where I ordered a cheeseburger, fries, and a cup of coffee to go. It was quiet, almost empty, blue and gold daylight pouring in through the front picture windows and reflecting off the polished floors and walls. When the barmaid brought me my order, I asked if Frank was around (from my reading I knew the bartender/owner of the Dunes was named Frank). I had seen him the night before at the other end of the bar, but there'd been no chance to approach him in all that noise and his work.

No, he won't be in today. But if you go up to the motel on the hill, you'll find him.

I drove up, parked, and walked into the motel's office, my manila envelope at my side. Frank came out from the back room to the counter and asked if he could help me.

Is Jim in town this weekend?

No, he's not. Was up last week.

Could you give him this the next time you see him? I held the crinkled and bulging envelope over the counter, my eyes steady, and assumed the most open and serious face I could. In several books I'd encountered the notion that to make it in life you would find yourself in situations where you had to act as if you belonged. If you acted natural, a part of the scene, and did not become overly conscious and show signs of being an outsider, others would accept you.

He took the envelope. He squinted at its blank face. Yes, I can.

I think we shook hands. I know I said thank-you, turned, and quickly stepped out of the office before he had a chance to change his mind. I wasn't sure what I expected to happen; this was the first time I had done anything like this. I floated in a strange elation to my van.

Back at Purdue days passed. The warm Indian summer of southern Indiana was over, all the colorful leaves had fallen, the days turned gray and rainy. I spent more time inside reading and writing. Then one day (out of the blue, as I heard growing up in Michigan) some three or four weeks after visiting Grand Marais, I was down at the Hawkins House post office and was given a large envelope, my name written in elegant cursive, and inside were all my manuscripts. None of the words or sentences was marked, nor were there any comments on the pages. There was another, letter-sized gray envelope addressed to me in the same cursive. My hands were trembling as I tore open the envelope and pulled out the typed letter on fine paper. I read it several times.

There were so many people who wanted to be writers, but there was nothing more difficult than writing, Harrison told me. And he doubted writing could be taught. A person who wanted to write better make sure it was necessary on a spiritual-emotional level because it was such a hard thing to do. He had read through my manuscripts and liked best the story that began with my grandmother cooking in her kitchen. He wrote that my prose showed promise but it was up to me to figure out what I wanted to do with it. I felt that he left me with a line to continue working with: *a tricky way of saying something unnecessary will not do* (words I recognized from his poem "In Interims: Outlyer"; and I added these as well: "Clear your speech, it is all that we have / aloud and here and now"). He made it clear that he could be of no help, and thus he didn't want to hear from me again.

The letter shook in my hands. Inside, my stomach and chest trembled. I had received some praise from teachers and student writers. I had never published a word. For years I had been called *stúpido*, belittled, had lived in apartments and houses that roared with my father's verbal and physical rage. Since the age of fourteen I'd worked seasonal and full-time jobs, and for the last five years had worked in a factory. Writing was a happy accident, a discovery I had no control over. I was too close to beginning to say it was saving my life. There was nothing of my life worth saving. But in that moment, trembling in front of the mailboxes, trying to steady my hands, I read the letter again and shook with new emotions, with the power of words.

For months I walked around with a question: *What's promise? What's my promise?* I had never achieved a thing, and was, accordingly, never good at anything. No one had ever promised me a thing, nor had I ever made any promises. I worked and felt it was a miracle at the end of the week that there was an envelope with a check made out to me, each time the nervousness in my stomach disappearing only when I had cashed the check and held the money in my hand. Then I spent it as fast as I could before anyone had the chance to take it away. And when the economy turned, I'd be laid off or no longer have a job. How could I promise a part of my life? What could I do? It was astonishing that Harrison liked best the story that began with my Abuela cooking; it was the first story I had ever written. I had returned to the story many times and revised it, but I always recognized those first and immediate words that arose of their own volition from memory and imagination. It was as if Harrison had the ability to pinpoint some truth in my writing, some truth from my life. How could he do that? He didn't know me. And why had I lived some dozen years not remembering Abuela?

Later it dawned on me what Harrison might have meant by "unique" and "tricky." Too many thought about becoming a writer and then yoked together the image of a writer with a unique personality, or thought that to be a writer required unique experiences. As if that was the trick, as if, too, writing was accomplished because of certain tricks that some people knew. And as if these tricks might exist because some wrote of things that were not necessary. They didn't write of what was essential, needed, and wanted—that is, essential for their whole being on an emotional-spiritual level. *Desire. Want. Yearning.* When you are writing you move temporarily from this world into another, you try to get as close as possible to this other world, this dream world set in motion by your desire, want, yearning. That's writing.

Don't put the cart before the horse. A notebook. To be utterly alone. To sit and stare hard at what is in front of you. Inside you. To watch horses running across a burnt cane field, to capture the colors and details, the smells and actions, the vividness of the moment imprinted across the ribbon of memory like red dust powdering a horse's hooves. To write it all down. To look at it again. Again you look at it. And then write again without worrying about where those horses are headed.

It has nothing to do with some idea of "the writer." There's nothing unique in this process, Harrison seemed to say, but it better be necessary. All alone I yearned to get closer to that young boy looking at his grandmother cooking in her kitchen, and as I wrote the images and details that had lived inside for so long, that writing had the promise of becoming something greater than who that boy was, or his memory.

I should never have attempted to meet Harrison. But I was crazy to write, crazy for consciousness, for language, and the possibilities of a writing life. I should never have intruded on his life. And I look back with great sadness because I was asking Harrison for validation and guidance, things I had never received from anyone else, so I might make the right choice. I didn't know better, I had no models or memories to guide me. Still, it was wrong. I was running on wonder, naiveté, and dreams. They were my necessary compass points toward a life I wanted to live, even if nothing in my life had seemed to prepare me for where I was going, how I might discover my true north. Harrison's words of promise became a small fire I had to shelter.

In these troubled times
I go inside and start a fire. ("Cabin Poem")

The Dunes Saloon was packed. Drinking, talking, laughing. Fat hamburgers, baskets of fried fish and potatoes, a steaming pizza on a silver pedestal in the middle of the table. The saloon bright, the lights reflecting off the colored bottles and the mirror behind the bar. I don't remember much, and because I never took notes or tried to write this story, and shared it only with friends, twenty years or more have passed and I can't recollect if I was at the Dunes Saloon one or two nights. Perched on a stool I was caught up in a kind of practice; taking in the tone of the light and how it might diminish in the back hall as a figure entered through the door. I watched and listened to the voices, focused on faces and clothes, tried to distinguish the locals from the visitors. As if the continual, almost feigned laughter of a man dressed in a pressed flannel shirt layered over a turtleneck sitting next to another man in a navy blue T-shirt, its collar stretched from many washings, a red, oddly shaped mark like a burn from a muffler or the scrape of rough bark on the side of his bicep, revealed something below the surface. How one man's vest had a torn pocket and shoulders streaked with oil and grease, and when he raised his beer to his lips I could see that his knuckles were tattooed by the oil and grease; and, at the next table, how a man wore a shiny yellow windbreaker, khaki pants, and leather boat shoes without socks, his ankles tanned. I outlined in my mind the shapes of bodies, the size of shoulders or stomachs, the growth of a beard, and zoomed in on the scuffmarks or lack thereof on the toes and heels of boots and shoes. How one man took his bottle or glass of beer slowly while the other never paused in drinking his whisky. The black tin ceiling shone, and I glanced at the dimples and ridges, the way the light streaked across the tin or pooled in soft gold, as if these might be details I'd need in the future. I felt feelings of memory in that saloon. I had to practice writing these things across the ribbon of my memory, for later when I would sit down and try to remember.

Three months before, I had arrived at Purdue University with around three thousand dollars. The process of getting a college degree, becoming a writer, was something I didn't fully understand. I would listen and observe, but I didn't have any design or purpose in mind, and thus no knowledge of what it might take to finish school and then make my secret dream of becoming a writer a reality. I was still dreaming. I wasn't sure if my savings would get me through the first semester, let alone the second. And once the money ran out, what then? All I had was the present, now, and maybe that kind of energy helps to explain why I wrote so much that fall. What was I looking for in that saloon? What was I practicing? Why was I spending money I didn't have to spend?

The older man on the next barstool started a conversation. He too was turned around and looking as if he were practicing. We started talking, faced the bar, and easily enough he bought me a drink, and then I bought him one, but he wasn't done with the drink in front of him so the barmaid gave him a wood coin for when he was ready for it. Before too long I had a wood coin. John had several front teeth missing and had lost most of his dirty-blonde hair and styled what was left in a comb-over, with long strands in the back touching his collar. He was tall and thin, his brown eyes bright, and he was a drinker—I could see it in his red bulbous nose, his trembling hand, and his breath that smelled of old wine and an overflowing ashtray. His fingers were crooked, his hands dry, cracked, and mottled with freckles, and though his right hand trembled as it approached his glass of red wine, once he lifted the glass toward his lips it became steady and sure. John asked what I did for a living and what I was doing up north. It was embarrassing to admit I was a college student—the first time I'd had the chance to say so—and thus I began in the past talking about my job for a bit, and how I had quit in August to attend Purdue. I learned that he had a cabin up on the ridge and some forty acres of timber. He said something to the effect that with my change in life at least I was headed somewhere. We were quiet. I may have nodded. We talked of fishing and he gave me some spots for trout. We laughed with drink. Before the night was over he gave me directions to his cabin and invited me to stop by the next day. Maybe we'd head over to the Two Hearted River.

That August, just before school started, Jill and I went up to Drummond Island for several days. On the shore of Lake Huron we set up our campsite looking to the west through islands and currents, the turquoise waters stirred by the breeze. We rode our bikes out on the alvar along the edges of woods and swamps. We swam in the lake's cold, clear water. On the shore of our campsite we took broken pieces of limestone and built a high fire pit and cooked up a pot of black beans with smoked habañeros, mango, cilantro, garlic, onion, cumin, and ham hocks. We made a side of guacamole, warmed tortillas, and opened a bottle of chilled white wine. The sun fell below a stand of thick pines, the islands and currents mottled with oranges and purples. We had our chairs close to the fire, the stones warmed by the dancing flames; the beans simmered away, and I read aloud from Harrison's "The Man Who Gave Up His Name." So much of my interior life was growing and changing, and I never wanted to leave a moment like this.

I had been introduced to Harrison's work that spring when reading his collection of novellas, *The Woman Lit by Fireflies*, in a fiction-writing class at IUSB (Indiana University–South Bend). I found and voraciously read Harrison's "The Raw & The Cooked" articles in *Esquire*. At Purdue I turned to his poetry, and on a trip to Chicago found several of his novels—*Dalva*, *Sundog*, *Wolf*—at a bookstore in Lincoln Park. Each week, beyond my required school reading, I made myself read at least one new book that had nothing to do with my classes. It all started to accumulate within me, and I felt the depth of a richly lived life, imagined a man living in his own diverse physical world. Even if the sweaty imprint of factory work was still palpable, I was beginning to feel cut loose, the inkling of freedom, which was thrilling and frightening. I missed the days of work, feeling productive, and the paycheck, but new things were building and moving me toward another life.

In one of Harrison's articles there was a savory recipe for menudo that ended with a strong recommendation: read Jimmy Santiago Baca's *Working in the Dark: Reflections of a Poet of the Barrio*. I had never heard of Baca but immediately ordered a copy at the bookstore and picked up two collections of his poetry: *Immigrants in Our Own Land* and *Martin & Meditations on the South Valley*. *Working in the Dark* arrived from Red Crane Press in Albuquerque, which might as well have been as distant as Paris or Madrid, and I felt as if I was the only one in the world, surely in Indiana, reading Baca's essays and stories. I devoured Baca's books and started to discover all the Spanish hidden inside me—the words and phrases of my childhood, a distant self of language, people, work, and song I had lost years ago.

At the same time, I had stumbled upon a reference for Clark City Press out of Livingston, Montana. All their books looked beautifully designed, and there were all these writers I now wanted to read, but it was Harrison's *Just Before Dark* that called my attention the strongest. I ordered a copy, and when it arrived I paid twenty-five dollars, the most I'd ever spent on a book. Every free moment I opened those cream-colored pages, the type and quality of paper so elegant and fine. An afternoon turned into evening, and time was not as important as the words I closely followed, held in my mouth, turned over and over like small stones, until they softened and I swallowed them like warm bread fresh from the oven. I sat at a café table with a notebook and a cup of coffee writing down images and sentences, sketching out ideas and memories, staring at the sky purpling in the twilight.

At the age of twenty-three I was being offered a glimpse into the possibilities of my rural Michigan life: the trees, rivers, and fields; fishing, hunting, and farm life; the cold and snow and gray and sad mood of winter, and the bright blue of early summer and self almost crazed with light, earth, and movement. Harrison offered me Spanish words and foods and regions—Key West, the Southwest, Mexico, Costa Rica, Brazil—that sparked new memories. He also introduced me to Federico Garcia Lorca, a life-changing gift, and I began reading his poems and explored his *duende* in *Deep Song and Other Prose*. It was a New Directions hardcover, brand new, ten dollars, yet dusty and abandoned on the bookstore shelf, and once again I felt as if I alone was reading Lorca's words for the first time. I penciled a small asterisk next to these mysterious, compelling lines:

"The figure of the cantaor is found within two great lines, the arc of the sky outside, and on the inside the zigzag that wanders like a snake through his heart."

Harrison's "A Natural History of Some Poems" became a touchstone of fact. I had never written poetry in my life, didn't have any formal framework for understanding poetry, but Harrison's natural history became a kind of field guide; it spoke with such power because of how the personal and the intellectual fused, how the imagination reigned, and how Harrison stood on the borders of insider/outsider because his poetics was always open to change and evolution.

"The dynamic quality of poetics itself comes from the idea that every poet worth the name wishes to forge a 'key to a style'—a way of expressing himself equal to his vision," Harrison writes.

I read the selections from his notebooks included in the history countless times. What did I know of poetry? Not a thing. But Harrison's words helped me to begin listening for the key, helped me to hear poetry in life, and as a field guide his words helped me to follow a map that led to distant fields, valleys, and streams I had never walked. He writes:

> You must often hate poetry to write good poems.
>
> Remember: vividness, lucidity, momentum. A poem should not resemble "poetry" too closely. The first impulse on reading a true poem is almost awkward. Lines should not be anticipated nor should a line be diffuse unless it conceals a jolt. Some sort of unexampled tension, not necessarily to be resolved, is characteristic of good poems. And not merely a tension purely of language but in the objects and their emotional equivalents. If a single line is to serve as a fulcrum it must be double sharp, hard, and lucid. The whole point about a short lyric is to make the moment durable.

Vividness. Emotional equivalents. Double sharp and *hard* and *lucid* and *durable* were my keys as I walked through life attentively. I wanted to write my own short lyrics, and thus I was suddenly mad with poetry, writing poem after poem. Just a year ago my days in the factory had seemed far from poetic, and yet here was all this passion and attention to write poems. I brought no poetic ideals to this writing; I was simply a lake lapping against a stone shore, a yellow leaf tumbling to the ground to join other leaves, a lone car driving on an empty road passing through marshes and swamps, a man walking on a thin trail as the sun falls through a birch forest. Perhaps I did have too much time on my hands—and too much hunger, passion, and openness to take in as much as I could.

Through the screen door I saw him lying on the couch, very still, his longish hair splayed over a velvet pillow, his right arm over his eyes. I knocked and without looking he swung his legs out and stood. *Come on in, Fred.* John sat down on the couch, swung his legs up, and lay back down. *Have a seat,* he said, and waved toward a rocking chair in front of a window. The pine walls and floors glowed with sun and shadows. I smelled butter and onions, something like nutmeg, maybe cloves, and bay leaf and thyme. The cabin took away the chilled morning air, wood crackling inside the stove. There was a cast iron Dutch oven on top. Is the pot to let moisture into the room? Yesterday, he told me, he had been out on a gravel road when he flushed a grouse and hit it. It would simmer all day with some onions, carrots, potatoes, and red wine, and he'd have a fine meal later this evening. He coughed. He sat up as if he were going to stand, only to point at the pot. He couldn't seem to stop coughing or catch his breath. He lit a cigarette, took a deep drag, and lay back down in a cloud of smoke. *They taste so damn good,* he said.

I rocked back and forth taking in the shadows on the wall. Rocking back I held the chair steady for a moment with the balls of my feet, looked out through the window toward the pines and the afternoon light filling the needles and then refracting into wide rays of golden light. John sighed. His forearm was over his forehead, and in the shadowed darkness of the cabin I couldn't make out his face.

The pot hissed softly on the stove. What did we have to talk about? I had no idea what I was doing there. I'd felt there was something unkind in not accepting John's invitation. I felt the same when someone at the factory asked me to go fishing or to get a drink; even if I didn't know him very well, I would go—why would I say no?

In the corner of the window the silvery filaments of a spiderweb were beaded with drops of dew, mosquitos and moths caught within, and crawling across a filament a spider as big as a quarter.

John spoke again. He didn't know what to do. He met a young man last spring and hired him to help cut timber in his woods. John had a shop out back where the timber was further cut and milled. He and the young man worked out a deal where the man would complete some logging for John, and in exchange, he could cut down some trees to mill and build his own cabin on John's acreage. Now the man lived with his girlfriend in the woods and was spending too much time working on his cabin. John paused, his arms at his sides. He wanted to kick them off the land but wondered if it was too late. *You try to help someone,* he said, *and this is what it gets you.* John needed him to cut and mill his timber; he needed the money. His retirement was turning into a nightmare.

The spider pulled at the papery wing of a moth until it ripped free from the web.

What could I say? What experience or knowledge did I have? All I could do was stop rocking, say *yes* or *hmm* every so often, and listen. The sun moved northwest across Lake Superior, the shadows slid across the floor, and I watched a blue jay hop from branch to branch in a pine. The room had darkened so much I could barely make out John's head, let alone his face; his forearm like a strip of yellow-brown wood floating over the end of the couch. The moment was as familiar as my open hands upturned on my lap, the lines crisscrossing my palms. I grabbed the chair's arms and rocked. How many times had I walked into the living room to find my father lying just so on the couch? Sometimes he was sleeping, sometimes the TV was on, and oftentimes he was passed out, a bottle of rum or Canadian whiskey in a paper bag tucked under the edge of the couch. I had learned early to move around the house quietly, to stay alone in my room, to cultivate silence while my mind held all the noises I couldn't make, all the words I couldn't speak.

One late afternoon I returned home because I had forgotten my girdle and hip pads. My father was lying on the couch with a blanket. He had just started working at a factory for $3.45 an hour. He had lost his driver's license for his third drunk-driving citation, and finding a job wasn't easy. He needed my mother to drop him off in the morning, and he'd get a ride home from a coworker or walk home. The TV was on, the volume silenced. I grabbed my girdle and pads. When I passed back through the living room I said I had to go and had come only to pick up my forgotten pads. He let out a breath.

A month or so before he had decided to quit drinking, and how could I know that this time he'd stay sober for the rest of his life? Why hadn't he quit ten or even five years before? When I was younger, without one foot outside my father's house, we might've still had the chance to talk. Why hadn't I understood that what existed between my father and me was just some simple math? He's in third grade, eight or nine years old, and then move forward to 1983 and he's thirty-eight or thirty-nine. Now subtract the childhood he never had and my father has already been working for thirty years. Lying on the couch, after all those years of work—and how many moves?—my father might have arrived at the end of the equation: exhaustion, resignation, defeat. The biggest number work always led to: 0.

Just before I closed the door he said, *Whose car you drive?* I looked to the end of the driveway. I started to turn around. I could have asked him to come to the game. He could've watched me play football for the first time. I gripped the knob, turned it, and as I pulled the door shut I said a friend let me borrow it.

Earlier that summer, in late August, I was driving to the lumberyard to begin my afternoon shift when my father passed me in the other lane. He was in the passenger seat of an unfamiliar car and there was a woman driving, her thick, curly hair blowing out the window. My father turned toward me just as I passed, and noticing the sharp twist of his neck, his hard jawline, I stomped down on the gas pedal. Less than a quarter of a mile to go. I thought if I made it to the next stop sign and quickly turned left, I could get away. But what was I speeding from? My father knew where I worked, and the only way to get away was to keep on driving down to the highway, turn north or south, and keep going as fast as I dared. Dust and gravel splashed against my tires and fenders when I pulled into the parking lot, threw it in Park, turned off the ignition, and jumped out. I hurried toward the loading dock. The gravel crunched, the car pulled in behind me, and the door creaked open and my father was yelling and slamming the door shut. His hands were trembling at his sides. He yelled: *Didn't you see me?* It must have been in the high nineties with the humidity just as high. He was swaying, the blue veins in his hands thick with anger, but what struck me the most were his red eyes, how he couldn't seem to keep them open and then suddenly they would jerk wide. He lifted his cap off his head. Sweat lined his forehead and ran along the back of his hands and forearms to where his blue chambray shirt was rolled just past his elbows, the edges of the cloth dark. He pulled his cap on tighter.

The car engine ticked. He had forgotten his house key that morning when he walked into town. The woman stuck her head out the window and smiled. I handed my father the key. He said, through gritted teeth, his words slurred by whiskey, something like, *Don't drive away, somna bitch, when you see me.* If I had been standing a few inches closer, if that strange woman wasn't in the car, I'm sure I would have felt his wet, hot fist driving into my face or stomach.

John's lighter flicked, the orange-blue flame high in the dark shadows of the living room. He let out a long, circling funnel of smoke. Rays of sunlight fell through the screen door and the front windows and pooled on the wood floor by my feet. The couch and the stove crowded the room. Over my shoulder, through the open window, a raven cawed somewhere out in the woods as the silence grew. The earthy, dark smell of the grouse simmering on the stove felt warm on my face.

On the other side of the door, just before I got in the car and drove back to the locker room, I heard my father's voice from the couch: *No insurance for you, Freddie. No drive.*

John coughed again, the crow cawed, and I thought I heard its wings flapping, followed by the simmering pot's light hiss.

What could I ever know of my father's life if I only heard his anger, if I only remembered his drinking, if I never listened to what he carried inside as he lay on the couch?

John's cigarette glowed.

I remembered for the first time how the blanket was pulled tight underneath my father's chin, how his jaw was set hard, and the white bandage across his cheek. A large splinter had broken from a crate and jumped from the assembly line and struck his face. What use was all that when an hour's pay—a measly $3.45—could barely buy a pint of whiskey?

It wasn't so much that I experienced an epiphany as that all the worry and pain I had carried around in my stomach as a child leapt up into my chest, wrapped itself around my heart, and then turned into my own splinter: it was thick and jagged and made of rage, and when it entered, the spasms were sharp and hot. *Three dollars and forty-five cents. Having to ask for a ride, having to make up some story for why you can't drive, looking around and deciding to just walk home.* My chest filled with burning waves, the rage and shame tumbled, crashed, and each wave became an image that flashed in my mind. One after the other they rose, tumbled, and crashed until they became one: a line of men walking down the side of a gravel road, each man linked by a rope that circled their waists. Juan, Raphi, Dracula, a man without a name holding a knife, and my father with his bandaged cheek. All those Puerto Rican men like my father who had worked and lived with a lonely, sad silence. Pain. Uncontrollable anger. Sometimes nothing but drunken laughter. I added John. They were all part of some story I might someday write, if only I could learn how to listen, if only I could follow the zigzag cutting through my heart.

John lay there with the back of his forearm over his eyes. I couldn't answer him or say anything significant as he wondered what to do with the man living in his woods. What answers did I have? I had closed the door on my father and run back to the car. What was I running from? Where did I think I was going? Who was I kidding—I could never escape from my father, could never leave him behind no matter how many times I tried to run away. Even in death he'd still be in my life, walking down a gravel road. The only way I could get away was to willfully forget, but then no matter how blank and dark my mind became, memory would have all the room it needed to come rushing back. I felt the afternoon moving toward evening, beckoning me to get up and come outside. I rocked a bit longer. I knew I had to write their stories even if I didn't know how, even if I didn't understand how many years it might take. I only felt I had to stay with them on the gravel road. All I needed to do was follow. All I needed to do was listen. I needed to look and look. And maybe I could give them a ride home.

*
**

Writing about this time in my life has nothing to do with affirming Jim Harrison's letter—nor am I trying to suggest I had some connection to him. I write about this moment because of the mystery that arose from his words. Why did he choose my story of Abuela cooking in her kitchen as holding the most promise? What did he see, read, or admire as *promising*? When Harrison opened my thick manila envelope and saw the many manuscripts he must have anticipated a long day of boredom. He must have read those immature, derivative, and false pages without any sense of urgency. Most of my writing must've been filled with grammatical mistakes. Pages and pages of errors as I tried to write in one language what had happened in another language. And yet that one story of my grandmother cooking in her kitchen spoke to him. Beyond the words on the page he heard some promise for my prose.

That memory and story of Abuela came from a place I'd never understood to exist within me. My father had taken me to Puerto Rico when I was eight or nine, and our two-week stay turned into a month, then six weeks. Those weeks, those days, the slow, lush hours, seared themselves into my memory, even if I went a dozen years without remembering them. The sweet sugarcane I cut from the field across from the house and eat every day. The mangoes, oranges, and little finger bananas I pick and eat until I am close to bursting. The way the red clay road sparkles and deepens under the bright sun. Muscular horses galloping across a burnt field. Hummingbirds. Bougainvillea. Hummingbirds. Orchids. A white ox. Hummingbirds with green heads and ochre throats drifting in and out of the kitchen's open window. Steam and song, Abuela dancing, her sandals scraping her tiled floor, and the shadows of palms shaking and striping the floor perfectly in time with her song, her dance, her spoon striking the side of a silver pot.

I was living in South Bend, Indiana, never with any ambition to become a writer, when one evening Abuela returned to me. Up in the attic apartment of an old Victorian, across the street from Notre Dame, sitting on an aluminum folding chair at a red card table, I remembered Abuela and wrote down the words that came to me in a blue-covered notebook. That was a story I had to listen to—a story I had to see, smell, taste, and touch into words.

Writing on that borrowed red card table I discovered something that has lasted more than anything in my life: in times of utter aloneness, when I become overwhelmed by feelings of boredom, indecisiveness, and wretched fear, I become more solid and sure because of the words I write. There's some hidden energy revealed in the attention given to and received from the words as they appear on the page and link together. Some compulsive or mysterious need draws me—magnetizes me—to the page, a scrap piece of paper, a notecard. I write the images and sensations without hesitation, without any thought between the slow, vivid pictures in my mind and my moving pen. Bursts of smells and colors and actions become whole paragraphs, and as I write them down they build into their own story.

That first story of Abuela had its own strange logic, a poetic experience arising from the memories I remembered, dreamed, and imagined. As the weeks passed I continued to return to the writing, adding and subtracting things, rearranging a few paragraphs, and slowly going over the words and sentences to see if I could hear what I had been offered.

What had I hoped for in looking for Jim Harrison in the Dunes Saloon? What did I expect to happen around 10:00 p.m. when he walked in the back door, took a table, and ordered a whiskey? Was

I naïve enough to dream that once I walked up, introduced myself, and said I was a writer he would ask me to take a seat? Maybe we would talk about life and literature. Maybe he'd invite me to hang around. He'd give me directions to his cabin, and the next day I'd go out there. In Harrison's presence—walking and looking, drinking and cooking, eating and talking—I'd encounter moments of wisdom that would change my life forever. Is that all I ever wanted—someone to talk to, someone to show some care, something that would help me to change—*reinvent*—my life? No. That can't be true because when I write I am utterly alone and I encounter a different, better self.

I know that in the end the letter Harrison wrote is meaningless. Who am I kidding—there may have been hundreds, if not thousands, of young writers who searched him out, discovered his address, and disturbed his life. Writing isn't a lottery. It isn't playing the numbers. It isn't a Friday evening in an abandoned lot next to a packaged liquor store, men in a half-circle tossing dice against a brick wall. There was no one who could ever let me know if the years of struggle would lead to anything. I was the only one who could discover my writing's promise.

A dark zero. The white bandage, the frayed strands of cotton around the edges. One day his thick head of hair silver white. I had gifted my father an elegant scrimshaw knife. The handle a clean cream with a trout rising for a fly in black carved into the bone (or maybe—it was so long ago—a pair of mallard ducks in flight against some cattails). From my father I had learned that the one thing you could always keep close and rely on is a machete or a knife. There were always fish or rabbits to clean, goat meat to cut up, sugarcane to cut and peel. One day at lunch he had gotten up from the break room table and walked to the bathroom to piss, only to discover on his return that his knife was gone. His sliced apple still sat on the table next to his plastic bowl of rice and black lunchbox, the coffee from his thermos still steaming, but the scrimshaw knife had disappeared.

Like me my father is a man of few words, one never to speak up, and as he looked around the table he didn't see anyone he could accuse of stealing his knife. Even when he spoke to the foreman all he could say was he returned and the knife was gone and ask if maybe someone had found it.

I wonder if in the days that followed he ate his lunch with his coworkers or took to sitting at an empty table. He never said anything to me about the knife. One morning over coffee my mother whispered how he was so upset. It had happened the first day he took it to work and he didn't have the heart to say anything.

I thought my father looked sad and resigned lying on that couch, sick as he tried to give up drink one last time. Maybe it was his poor job. Maybe it was the splinter that cut his face. I had forgotten about the knife; it never entered my mind. Then the white bandage, the splinter, the flecks of silver beginning to show in his mustache—the knife, its bone handle, the carved image returned to me. I must've wanted to give or tell him something; I must've wanted him to recognize something between us. I don't know what I wanted because I can't recollect what I felt in buying the knife. All I can recall is my father on the couch, the blanket pulled up over his shoulders, close to his chin, and the white bandage across his cheek.

*
**

There were still a good four or five hours of daylight left when I drove out to the Two Hearted River. Out of Grand Marias I took the Adams Trail, a slow-going gravel road to Lake Muskallonge, and then turned northeast to arrive where the Two Hearted met

Lake Superior. It was late afternoon. The birch and beech trees were golden with leaves and the sun moving to the northwest. Trailers were being backed down the ramp to load up boats. There was loud talk and the booming bang of aluminum, the slosh of water being dumped, dripping on the ground. I crossed the small bridge over the river to a long edge of beach littered with colorful stones and agates—red and black, white flecked with tan and green and red, various tones of silvers and grays and blues. The Two Hearted was small, perhaps even unremarkable as rivers go, and no one was fishing near the mouth. The beach was deserted and pleasant just for me, the trees stirring in the wind, the smell of a wood fire spicy and turning me warm inside, a chill rising along my arms as I walked the shore. Out in the distance a red-and-white freighter slowly glided west. The smoke and the sea winds filled me, and I listened to the waves rush over the colorful stones. I felt something that would not come to me in words. It couldn't be named hunger, regret, or even excitement. Some new kind of *dreaming* and *longing*—that's what I felt, and with those feelings I stood hard, balanced, all alone. I knew then I needed to return to Purdue. I had to continue reading, writing, and learning who I might become.

On my walk back I stopped in the middle of the bridge. Looking north I followed the freighter until it disappeared from sight, the sun beginning to strike the horizon, the crashing waves purpling with twilight. *Sure is beautiful,* I heard someone say. Up on a dune of beach grass and pines there was a heavyset man in a brown coat, his dark skin almost the same color, mustached, his left eye squinting. He was wearing a fishing cap, his ankles crossed as if meditating, looking hard toward the horizon. *Sure is,* I said, and followed the Two Hearted until it met the sea.

Walking the trail back to my van, my stomach and chest were light and free. I stepped up into the driver's seat, closed the door, and started down the gravel road toward the highway. Sitting on the dune the man had seemed to exist with an assurance or trust in his aloneness. I wanted to stay there, was beginning to learn the significance of sitting still without a care for time and staring hard at the things that could not care less for my attention. The leftover trees from a recent fire were skeletal and black like strongly inked lines across the plain. Wondering how long he might stay there, I drove on and considered how distances begin to disappear in the last moments of daylight. I could touch the sky, gather the emerging stars that pierced the evening's blue, the tops of the still, straight and charred trees silvering in the fading light.

When I turned southeast toward home, hit the blacktop road, the moon of a lifetime rose—round, huge, blue-white above the glowing birch trees. I descended a hill into the Seney swamps and felt close to the earth as all sense of direction and movement fell away and I floated across the swamps and the moon became liquid and poured itself from the sky in watery light: flooding the trees and swamps, the road, my hands. I turned off my headlights, let the night pull me forward, and a sea of light carried me toward the place I most needed to find.

Next Country

A false start. To write memory is to select, to know that what is chosen is often accidental, and it leaves out other moments we carry within us, moments that help to define our gestures, shape our words. Memory: the invention of a story. I write one only for another to seemingly appear from thin air with urgency. "There are no depths, only distances," Guy Davenport writes. "Memory shuffles, scans, forges. Freud's geological model implies that last year is deeper in memory than last week, which we all know to be untrue. The memories we value are those we have given the qualities of dream and narrative, and which we have invented" (*The Hunter Gracchus*). Memory stories; it changes, it migrates and reveals another self that shapes my imagination.

Books held no value in my family. My mother attended night school to get her GED. My father had only a third-grade education. As if in a dream I enrolled as an English major at Purdue University in the fall of 1992. My parents had no advice, wisdom, or financial means to help me. I had spent the previous eight years working many jobs: grocery clerk, gas station attendant, water-well driller, carpenter's helper. A few months before attending Purdue, I worked a twelve-hour night shift in a factory. Now I had all this time on my hands and I worried over how to survive beyond the first year on the three thousand dollars I had saved. There were moments of boredom, whole days when I didn't know what to do. Sometimes I would begin to sweat, my stomach queasy, as I experienced what must have been some kind of shame because for the first time I could do whatever I wanted. I wasn't standing in front of a time clock.

That November I would turn twenty-six. After two years of classes at a community college and a small university, I moved from South Bend, Indiana, down to West Lafayette to attend Purdue full time. I wanted to write, but nothing in my life seemed to offer the possibility, imagination, or gift of language for writing; it was if I were moving to another country with only the clothes on my back. At the age of twenty-two I had discovered a love for words, lost days reading them, spent bright mornings writing them. (Later I would encounter Jean Rhys—"For I know that to write as well as I can is my truth and why I was born" [*Letters: 1931–1966*]—and look back at that young man, what he wanted, what I still want, what we keep moving toward.)

A mysterious energy arose from the page as I composed small paragraphs and vignettes. My childhood returned to me in motion. Hartford, Connecticut. Niles, Michigan. Añasco, Puerto Rico. Back to Hartford and off to Michigan once more. These places sprang to life and with them people whose voices and words and actions were vividly imprinted in my memory and imagination. There was texture to this life, strands of work, migration, music, food, and languages I didn't know how to weave together. For the first time in my life—free of my father's alcoholism, free of the poverty and unpredictability of my childhood—I felt a sense of purpose. I wanted to write, and I needed someone with more experience to help me know what I had to do to become a writer.

When I first tried to meet writer and teacher Patricia Henley at Purdue University, an adviser had recommended I inquire about enrolling in one of Patricia's fiction workshops. But when I called the English department I mistakenly remembered the name as *Beth* Henley. I asked if she was in. It was the middle of summer, and of course she was not in, and there was no "Beth" Henley. Perhaps I was looking for Patricia Henley? Some of the first writing I had ever done was a play on a manual typewriter, and maybe that caused me to remember the playwright's name. I was told to wait until fall classes began to talk to Patricia Henley.

When I went to meet Patricia that fall I was much too eager, perhaps even rude. With a stack of story manuscripts in hand, I stood outside her afternoon class waiting for it to end. The door opened, students streamed out, books against their chests or sides, pencils or pens between fingers, talk growing louder in the hallway. There was a break in the current and I squeezed through the door, stopping the line for a moment. Patricia stood at the podium straightening papers and talking to some students. I didn't wait for them to finish. I rushed up, my manuscripts held high, ready to talk fiction writing. I told her I had been writing for the past year, had just started at Purdue, and wanted to keep writing. I waved my manuscripts as I spoke. I don't remember if she took them to read. I want to say it was then—standing there at the podium, listening to my crazy/passionate talk—that she said I could join her spring workshop.

That fall I became even more driven to write. I attended classes, put in the hours of reading and studying necessary to complete my schoolwork. Every morning I was up at dawn, showered, and ready to go. Outside, in the cold morning air, I sat on the Memorial Union steps reading and writing in a notebook. After a day of classes and studies I would sit until twilight at an outdoor café table and over a few cups of coffee read some more fiction or a book of essays and write whatever my imagination turned toward.

That fall's golden light lasted forever. At one point I wrote a short novel in four days.

I met with Patricia a few times to discuss writing and writers. I often had no idea what I was trying to do or express. All I wanted was a life of writing *now*. I didn't appreciate all the reading and writing I still needed to do, the years of apprenticeship required to make this life of writing a reality. I shared my confusing thoughts and feelings with Patricia. I said something like, *I'm not sure this is for me. I'm thinking about leaving.* Her eyes and face were hard, serious. She said something like, *Well, it wouldn't be the worst thing in the world. Going out and working never hurt a writer.* Patricia let me know that I needed to choose what was best for me, especially if I felt I didn't belong. She was giving me the freedom to decide. No one was stopping me. That scared me. Just two months before, I had quit my full-time job. If I left Purdue I had nowhere to go. Outside Patricia's office I felt even more unsure, frightened by my choices.

My love for words may have started with a garage sale. It was a Saturday, I had stopped by to see Jill, who was helping her mother at the sale, and I, as a garage sale kid, looked around. There were some old magazines spread out on the ground, a Picasso print of Don Quixote, and a copy of Ernest Hemingway's *The Sun Also Rises*, the Scribner's paperback edition with the lovely painting of the rolling hills, the white farmhouses with red-tiled roofs, the bright blue sky and big yellow sun. I think Jill's mom gave it to me for free, and maybe I hung around the sale for a time, maybe I looked around some more. What I remember the most is heading to the back of the house, to a brick-and-concrete patio under a circle of tall trees, where I sat down on a black wrought-iron chair and started to read.

I will always remember that warm late-spring afternoon. The sun fell through the trees onto my hands, the pages of the book mottled with sunlight and shadows. I was wearing a new light blue oxford shirt, buttoned and tucked in, the sleeves folded back to my elbows, a pair of khakis. I felt rested, strong, and warm in this garden of words and images, sounds and smells, so far away from my hands sore with work, my mind bored and dazed by repetition and the deafening roar of machinery. I leaned back, held the words on the page close, as if seeing the words for the first time. Something as simple and ordinary as the description of quotidian actions and the physical atmosphere became incredibly powerful and affirming:

> In the morning I walked down the Boulevard to the rue Soufflot for coffee and brioche. It was a fine morning. The horse-chestnut trees in the Luxembourg gardens were in bloom. There was the pleasant early-morning feeling of a hot day. I read the papers with the coffee and then smoked a cigarette. The flower-women were coming up from the market and arranging the daily stock. Students went by going up to the law school, or down to the Sorbonne. The Boulevard was busy with trams and people going to work.

I wasn't as much taken to a different place through this language as returned to what mattered in my life: an active, sensual, working life found in the particulars of existence and place. In this passage from *The Sun Also Rises* everything is *fine*—the morning, the gardens, the smell of coffee and cigarette smoke, blooming trees, flowers. The feeling of warm brioche in my hand, the air of the day beginning on my arms, on my brow. Fingers touching paper, ink. People working, walking to school. I liked the smells and sounds, the images, and the physical sensations and details—there was something material in the words (regardless of the setting and storyline) that had the feeling of work. Life feels special in these details, in these words, and these particulars suddenly made my reading and life special—the life I had come from, the life I was beginning.

Reading that book set in motion new regions in my mind. I lost most of my Thursdays because of working the twelve-hour night shift on Tuesdays and Wednesdays, and then returning again on Saturdays and Sundays. Fridays were my free day. I woke very early, 4:00 or 4:30 a.m., and immediately stepped into the shower. I always wore clean khakis, a nice button-down shirt, and, depending on the weather, either black and cordovan leather dress shoes or white Sperry Topsiders. A brown flannel-lined barn coat finished my Friday ensemble. I would stop at the 7-11 for coffee, swing by and pick up Jill, and by 5:00 a.m. we were heading up to northern Michigan, maybe three or three and a half hours on the road. Once there, we drove around the lakes, followed country roads through the woods, stopped at a general store or next to a field of freshly cut hay in Horton's Bay. We'd visit Walloon Lake, Harbor Springs, and Traverse City. Sometimes we walked along a road taking in the cottages on the lake. In Harbor Springs we strolled down the small street of shops, looking in the windows, eventually stopping at some café for coffee and a sandwich.

It was on these road trips that I picked up several of Hemingway's books and read them. I had no knowledge of who he was, what others thought of him, why one should read or not read him. Whenever I mentioned Hemingway to my peers, their faces would change—mouth quirking halfway between a smirk and a smile, a moue of disgust, or laughter at my naiveté. Somehow, growing up in Michigan, growing up in America, I must have come across his name before—but it was then, at the age of twenty-two, that I discovered Hemingway's writing without the weight of memory and without a care for what anyone else thought.

Alongside my work I continued to read, and I was fascinated and saddened by *In Our Time* and *The Nick Adams Stories* because I had lost so much in not having read them when I was younger. The trips continued, even though I wasn't sure what I hoped to touch if ever I caught up with Hemingway's ghost on some northern Michigan road. All those drives blur together. They are rather mundane and simple, unremarkable, and certainly sentimental. Each trip seemed to end at some roadside restaurant or tavern, a steak dinner, a bottle of red wine, and long conversations about the day, my dreams of living in small house in the North Country, conversations that I wished could go on forever. I was for the first time falling in love with words and life, trees and lakes and streams, the way the sun glinted on the road as it set. And I was falling in love with Jill. She was helping me to transform my life. She was always commenting on the many magazines and newspapers I read, how I could do something with that reading instead of working in a factory, and maybe, in fact, could go to school. She must have also noticed how I was gleaning places and incidents from Hemingway's writings and life and then taking them to shape our drives up north.

One day, Jill was studying for an exam in her art class. I wanted her to spend the day with me—and she said no, she had to study. I imagined that maybe I could do something, maybe persuade her to leave her books behind and go out into the day. I picked up her book, skimmed the beginning of the chapter, some of the headings, and the conclusion. I suggested some key terms and definitions Jill might be asked and said there would most likely be an essay question, something like, "What are the three major tenets of Modernism?" I offered a scenario for how Matisse, Monet, and Picasso could help Jill write her essay. I don't know how or what I was imagining; it was my single-mindedness that always created passionate convictions, necessary fictions that got me through life. Jill went out with me that day, and when she took her exam she found that my reading helped her, the exam went fine, and she was even more convinced that I should do something with my reading, that I could go to college. Eventually, she talked me into enrolling in an English course at the local community college. And then, a few years later, she convinced me to quit my job and move to West Lafayette and attend Purdue University.

That summer, on one of our trips north, Jill and I discovered a stretch of beach outside Ludington, the sand a clean and soft tan, and we started to go there each week, amazed that there were never any footprints in the sand. When we drove up to the beach, I would make a U-turn and pull over on the top of a dune under a giant beech tree. We'd walk down the dune into a private bowl of sand, the focus of Lake Michigan's vast blue scintillating light. We'd set up our chairs and blanket and spend the day reading and swimming. Sometimes I'd blow up a rubber dinghy and carry it north along the shore, and then we'd launch into the freshwater sea and let the current and waves carry us south. Down the road from our beach was a red general store that had wooden iceboxes with brass hinges and handles. They sold Molson IPA in a blue-and-red paper box, six achingly cold bottles. I always brought a lobster in the cooler, maybe a pound of shrimp, some black beans, a few avocados, and a watermelon. In the late afternoon we drank cold beers, and at twilight I started the grill and simmered the black beans and boiled seasoned water for the lobster or shrimp. On a cutting board on top of the cooler I made guacamole—avocados, chopped jalapeno, onion, cilantro, smashed garlic, cumin, and lime juice. As the sun became a burning globe on the horizon, orange-pink as it touched the water, we took warm tortillas from the grill to make lobster or shrimp tacos with guacamole, had a bowl of black beans with a spoonful of sour cream on top, and more ice cold IPA.

Some afternoons all I did was read on the beach. My eyes followed the character and story, turning page after page, memorizing new words I wanted to look up in the dictionary and discover how they might populate my writing. I'd finish one book, take it up to the van, and return to my chair with a new one.

In "The Theory & Practice of Rivers" Jim Harrison writes,

> It is not so much that I got
> there from here, which is everyone's
> story: but the shape
> of the voyage, how it pushed
> outward in every direction
> until it stopped:
> roots of plants and trees,
> certain coral heads,
> photos of splintered lightning,
> blood vessels,
> the shapes of creeks and rivers.

Jill was the daughter of a doctor, everyone in her family was college educated, and her life seemed destined for someone much better than I was. Working class, living paycheck to paycheck—I had nothing to offer or promise Jill. How was it that we were introduced one evening, started talking, and then developed a friendship that blossomed into love? There's nothing I can explain or share with anyone else about this voyage—I must accept that I am a creek and continue to follow and learn its shape. I seem to have inner currents coursing to my true north, my North Country, and that is a region that is more palpable and beautiful because of Jill's presence. What Jill and I were doing in northern Michigan is clearly deeply intertwined with my reading and memory of Hemingway; there were affections we continued to follow and search out, my life sensually unfolding alongside his written pages. Unwittingly, as we traveled more and more to northern Michigan we were deepening my romance with language as well as our romance. Jill helped me to imagine and remember how my experiences could be a part of what Hemingway wrote as well as what he didn't write. The English language became new again, and at the age of twenty-two I started to understand the power of language. I started to read with enthusiasm and purpose; more important, I started to write the first pieces of memory—my first impressions—that are still a part of the books I am writing now. Somehow, the sun also rose for me, and my literacy was beginning to write the dawn of a life I was beginning to live.

*
**

Why had I decided to talk to Patricia? In the hall, just a few steps from Patricia's office, I tucked Jim Harrison's letter back into the envelope and slid it between some pages of *Just Before Dark*. There are some things you cannot share with others, even your closest friends. There are secrets you must struggle with. My upbringing, being a first-generation college student, and my work were experiences I couldn't easily confess. I couldn't envision how my past was relevant to my learning, writing, and life. I had never had any guidance about such things, and I felt I had to hide who I had been in order to make the leap into a college education.

To get me through this period of intense self-doubt, I suppose I needed the help of an experienced and mature writer, someone who could help me see the value of my words. Someone who would encourage my writing. Someone who wouldn't allow me to make excuses. Patricia became that someone. As my mentor, she filled my days with possibilities for reading and writing, and she challenged me to do whatever it took to live a writing life.

Patricia began each class by reading a writer's words or an anecdote of biography from a daily calendar, and this small act provided a glimpse into the unstoppable history and life of the written word. In workshops she read from a story—a passage, a few sentences—to illustrate an important element of craft for that specific day. She introduced me to writers like Raymond Carver, Andre DuBois, Richard Ford, and Katherine Anne Porter. It meant the world to encounter writers who were grappling with the burdens of family, class, and work. I sensed authority and authenticity in each of the writers Patricia introduced; they, too, struggled with place and identity, and in ways I wanted to understand. Katherine Anne Porter, for example, wrote beautifully detailed and compelling stories set in Mexico, which she described as her "much-loved second country." Porter was but one of the writers who helped me think about writing in exciting and new ways. She sparked connections and metaphors across borders and countries, so I could begin to remember and imagine how my childhood, in the shadows of the Puerto Rican House, contained a second country I would learn to love. A second country I needed to write into existence.

Back then I was a sponge and a songbird. I took in everything I read and held it close. I was exploring, learning, practicing, and the best way to begin as a writer is by playing another writer's music. Patricia listened carefully, and she heard my emerging style and voice, my music. She read every manuscript I gave her—too many to count, too many I should've held on to. My lyricism was often unbounded, which led me to write long, complex sentences. When I enrolled in college at the age of twenty-three, I struggled with English proficiency and grammar. I never felt that Patricia saw these as problems. Instead, she helped me hone my skills so that my sentences possessed more elegance, grace, and power. I can still recall how much creativity I gathered as Patricia took me through the use of em dashes and semicolons, both of us hunched over the sentences of Alice Munro, Richard Ford, and William Trevor. Through this kind of reading and writing she taught me the joys of the craft, the solitary pleasures of exploring the life of a sentence, and the sea change you experience when you are able to identify and touch in your mind what Raymond Carver called a writer's "unmistakable signature." She affirmed my love of words, reminded me why I loved to work with them and how a love for words is not enough to become a writer.

Recently Patricia wrote in a letter:

> You were on my mind this morning because I find that I'm starting my novel over again. You stand out as a writer who is always willing to do that. There's no way around it.

Most of my days of late lack purpose; they don't burn with the lyricism, passion, and magic that used to propel me into writing. I'm digging deeper into that old secret, into who I was and how it is that I've become a writer who has one foot in the North Country and one foot in the Caribbean, a writer caught between two much-loved countries. In writing these essays and memoirs, I've lost the mask of my invented characters and narrators, and to stare at the blank page without them is a great challenge of emotion, vision, and language. I find that the past is filled with too much loss, too many wasted years, a younger self I cannot save. I write images and memories that flounder in a turbulent sea. Too often the pieces I write seem fitful, false, freighted by the effort. It's as if my many years of writing have been a lie because I can't seem to trust the process, can't trust that the writing itself is the way. I question every decision, write pages that seem worthless. I know I have a story to share, but then there's always this other voice asking, *Who really cares about that story?*

Patricia once wrote at the end of a manuscript words I will never forget. *Just keep doing what you are doing.* She meant that I should continue reading with passion, writing the characters and places that matter to me, and imagining writing as an act of discovery. That's what I've always believed. My writing teaches me how and what I am writing. As I write today, here she is, my mentor once again, sitting beside me as I look over the sentences, telling me I know how to begin, that all I need is to just keep doing what I am doing.

A few years ago Patricia retired from teaching. She sent me a package. When I opened it, I was surprised and moved to find a beautifully framed photograph of Ernest Hemingway. She always found his writing an unfailing source of inspiration, work ethic, and craft. I once shared with her that when I was beginning to dream of writing, I would spend days reading Hemingway and chasing his ghost up in the northern Michigan towns and woods of his youth. In the photograph Hemingway is slim, moving closer to death, wearing a plaid wool shirt. He's in Idaho, in 1959. He's standing next to a dresser that has a specially made top so he can, as he did for years and years, stand while writing. He's holding a pencil in his right hand and his left arm is resting against the manuscript pages, the sentences he's working on visible. I imagine those beginning-to-curl pages are from *A Movable Feast*. In his face, in his stance, I feel the magic of writing. Looking at the photo I remember, as if it were a dream, sitting in Patricia's office on the fourth floor of Heavilon Hall and Hemingway up on the wall. He looks on as Patricia and I move through sentences clear and swift as a cold stream, lush and rolling like a green summer field.

Hemingway now gazes down on my writing table. When I glance up at him I remember Patricia's many gifts, am grateful that some twenty-two years later she is still my mentor and friend. Patricia fostered and affirmed my writing life. She helped me hone and craft my lyricism, develop my written art, and deserve my dreams. As I write, those who came before look down with encouragement. I can look up at the photograph, reread a letter, take a book off the shelf, sit here with the early gold light spilling over the fir trees and remember. Together, we move toward the next country.

Album

I told the boy that as far as I knew everything was rented. The van he had stepped from was caked with dust, the windshield streaked from the wipers' arc, the headlights speckled with bugs. A woman tilted her head out the passenger window and a man leaned back from the wheel, his face covered in shadows. The boy asked again, told me they had come up from Texas and they were sharing a trailer with another family on a farm in Brookston.

The farmer told us to find a place. Do you know any numbers for the trailer parks? He swung his arm out toward the highway and the cornfields and trailers. *We can only keep working if we find our own.*

I wanted to help. It was Sunday, and all I could think to do was get the phone book.

A small scar traced the underside of his right eye. He had short, slick hair, and he was dressed in a nice striped T-shirt and jeans. The boy stood determined, his face too serious (he may have been eight or nine), the parking lot hot and silent. I looked under Trailer Parks, under Apartments. The thin yellow pages might as well have been printed in a dead language. The names and numbers were meaningless; I couldn't connect any of them to the trailer parks and apartments out here on Highway 52.

The boy squinted, the cut of his bangs lying just above his eyebrows. I told him I couldn't find a number. *Maybe if you go inside a trailer park, there's an office. You could ask about any trailers for rent.*

He thanked me and turned back to the van.

I told him no problem—something like *not to worry, it was no bother at all.* In Spanish I said things: Spanish voices and words and smells and tastes welled up in me, and I had to speak, I needed the boy and his parents to hear I wanted to do something. His mother and father looked at me. She held up her hand and said, *Gracias.*

That May I had finished my first year at Purdue University. With my transfer credits I was now two semesters away from becoming the first person in my family to graduate from college. That summer there were things—memories, voices, words—turning within me like a tractor crossing a field, warm dust churning in my thighs and rolling up through my stomach, and when the tractor swung around to cross the field again, a wave of feeling billowed across my chest and ran down my biceps, and I was flooded with an energy I needed to harness. I spent all my time reading and writing, had begun to dream about graduate school, and Jill and I had visited the University of Montana. I wanted to touch beyond words the magic I had felt in *The Real West Marginal Way, Winter in the Blood,* and *A River Runs through It.* I was already beginning to intuit that I was embarking on a wonderful luxury: writing, reading, and more writing. It was clear that I could make something out of words equal to sweating in a factory or walking behind a tractor and bending in a dusty field to pick up potatoes and toss them on a wagon.

As a child I was a shy and quiet boy, and loud voices clashed in my head. I struggled to calm them, find some silent place for my Spanish and English. My stomach always hurt—waves of butterflies banging against my ribs—as I became anxious. Now I want to be reflective and smart, say that being bilingual may have been a gift, and yet for all the language I had, I was linguistically confused. And in trying to learn everything in English, I was a difficult, terrible student.

Those ugly butterflies: I see a young boy sitting on his bed, his fists striking his thighs and then punching his stomach, just under his ribs, as he tries to forget his fluttering stomach. I couldn't understand why my father was always angry and drunk. He had chosen to live in this small town so far from home, and it seemed to cause him nothing but misery. When my stomach hurt, I'd become sad and confused and scared. Deep down, I knew, it was all my fault for being in trouble at school too much, for reminding my father that he never had a childhood.

That Sunday morning I had risen early, spent some time writing, and then I returned to my reading of Richard Ellmann's *Yeats: The Man and the Masks.* My biggest care that day was the heat; it was in the high nineties, humid, and I was just about to leave and drive one hundred miles to Lake Michigan. I knew there would still be work in my future, but that summer I took a step toward giving myself fully to what I saw as this other, foreign life. No matter how foolish, no matter how hungry, no matter how much worry, no matter how much failure I might encounter—I wanted a new life. I wanted to discover how to bring together those voices, how to release that wave of butterflies into a colorful garden of words.

Still, there were parts of my childhood no one should ever know. I was afraid of my younger self, had been taught to be ashamed of and to forget that boy, and I never wanted to see a portrait of that self in my writing. I had learned to hate my language—my un-Castilian Spanish, my often ungrammatical, verbose English, an English some university professors described as a turgid translation. I began in college as a remedial writer and wondered: *How will you ever become a writer?* Then my reading saved me. Silence and isolation. Reading the days away, long nights under lamplight. The loss of memory like erasing a blackboard or crossing out all the sentences on a sheet of paper with heavy red lines. Over time I discovered a language beyond the hate and shame: paragraphs, vignettes, poems, fictions—I was mad to write them all. And in writing page after page, I heard a lyrical voice and found the power of the written word to transform life.

Now I had a chance to help that boy become more than his memory.

For a moment, perhaps when the van's license plate blurred and became illegible in the distance, I must have recognized within myself a boy who had once loved to read and write, who was curious to learn anything, only to become withdrawn, silent, and then like his father accept a life of work. I see my younger self sitting at a table in a library, my hands and eyes exploring the thin pages of an encyclopedia. Each page turns crisply, like touching a thin fall leaf, and the printed words are bold, hard, and loud, stamped on my fingers and palms, imprinted forever in memory. A whole universe in one letter—*aardvark, Argentina, asp, anchovy, apple, Andalucía.*

The van turned west on the highway. I felt the humidity build, walked around in a rush, now unsure of the drive to Lake Michigan. The van continued down the highway and I came closer to things I thought I had left behind: roughly twelve years before we had stopped at that market out on US 31, and from some need I couldn't express, I tried to save my father from his drinking and asked the farmer if my father and I might work there.

I stand there once again looking out on the highway, remember the warm sweat running down my back, the van in a cloud of dust, begin to follow the boy's story, begin to remember that he was—an eight- or nine-year-old boy—asking about a place for his family to live so they could continue working on a farm. I wish I could remember every word he said. Wish I could've recorded them. Wish I'd returned to my apartment and written it all down. The moment was fleeting, shocking. He had said they needed a place to stay so they could continue working. He had said they were sharing a trailer with another family. But now, in memory, the word *four* continues to return. Under that hot Indiana sun four families went out in the fields, and when they came home they shared one trailer.

There are days when I still wonder what happened to the boy's family. Did they find a place? Did they stay in Brookston? Where did they go to work and live? There might have been a late-fall morning when his parents told him they were leaving. I see his last day of school: he walks across the schoolyard, hears the other boys yelling in a game of football, passes through the shadows of the monkey bars, and feels like a leaf being pushed and tumbled by the wind.

Every time I turn a page, steal a moment to write a few words, I remember that boy. Face the evidence of the boys and young men who travel dangerous distances. South America, Central America. Wonder how, like my father (like countless fathers and mothers, aunts and uncles), how can they begin working at such a young age. Small, dying Midwest towns brought back to life as Latin@s create a home. All these lives and migrations with and without words. How to express the pain of being deported back to a country you never knew, since the United States is your home? How to express 2,500–6,000 children separated from their families, sent thousands of miles away to a chain-link cell, a thin reflective sheet for the night as they cry for their mothers and fathers, cry in fear for not knowing where they are, why they've been taken away? How, out in the moonlight, how to place your ear to the ground and listen?

If this writing could find its way toward a memoir that contains their lives, I would also have to compose a meditation on *why I write*. And in that meditation I recognize that writing is an embrace—*un abrazo fuerte*—discovered through an act of witness. Or, better yet, listening. Listening for the lyrical place, the ground of song, *canto hondo*, inside/outside fences. To sow the peoples, places, and stories—the words—into the earth. To break open a small furrow near the heart so others will finally listen. A small furrow that contains earth, seed, water. Life, lives.

In California there's a young man who knows hardly anything about his family's live-in housekeeper. All he knows is her first name, Carmen. In one of his university classes he's given an assignment. Wonders if he can interview Carmen. He learns of her hunger and poverty as a child, her migration to the USA, and the violence she endures here. (Maybe he wonders more: *Was your journey a dream or a nightmare, Carmen?*) She tells him there was a day when she decided she must change her life. She begins working three jobs to help her brother go to school. Now Carmen works six days a week. She is given a small room to sleep in. A housekeeper until the seventh day, when she visits her family. The young man tries to thank her. Carmen thanks him. Why? "Because every night I come up to my room and I lie on my little bed," she tells him, "and I tell myself the story of my life—just in case someone should ever ask."

Carmen's story is a story shared by many (the sociologist Barbara Myerhoff and the poet and essayist Christine McEwan have shared it before). I've come to recognize that I am part of a generation that is trying to share Carmen's story, trying to make her life and story matter. At the same time, we are trying to tell the story of our lives—just in case someone should ever ask, just in case some day people decide to listen. Carmen's story resonates with me because it seems such a part of why I write, part of the peoples and characters I try to let live on the page. When I feel like I have nothing to write, no one to write to, I imagine more of Carmen's story.

*
**

I'm sitting at a wide, gleaming table in the Purdue University library. A large book with a yellow-and-black cover that contains photographs of Latin America is open in front of me. The accompanying text is in German, but that doesn't matter because the photos gather all my attention. I should be studying for a class, writing a paper, yet I can't leave this geography of places and peoples. A topos of memory and history both familiar and strange in the glistening lined faces, a wagon stacked with stones making its way along a road freshly blasted and carved around the edge of a mountain, ancient ruins slowly being swallowed by a jungle. Peasants in white standing amid vast rows of banana trees, on the edge of lush forests, out bending in fields, or walking down dirt roads that go on forever toward the horizon.

The mise-en-scène of work: wagons and carts and bundles of cane, gray-black swirls of smoke, and a mill's brick smokestack rising into a cloudless sky.

The silver gelatin photos light up the table, details shining with liquid clarity. I love the figuration of black and white, shadows and light like a curtain in an open window softly pushed by the breeze. I sit for hours looking at these photographs that quiver lucidly on the page, the borders of the book disappearing as a photo becomes a cave, a tunnel, a flat clear pool. I dive: liquid, warm, floating in a world of vision and dream and utter stillness.

I am a child running through my father's barrio, chasing a lizard across the cool patio, cutting a piece of cane with a machete, following the sun as it slowly moves across the red dirt road, the mountain's green thickening with blue shadows. These photographs open a new window of memory: the snap of soapy water flung from a tin bucket against cobblestones, the low huff of an ox lumbering across a field, the thud of a breadfruit falling to the ground. Then another, followed by another, and in between, the silence grows with the slow whirring of an emerald hummingbird outside the window. A boy might stand in a moment like this forever.

I open my notebook and begin to compose stories. There isn't a whole story—there's too much absence in any photograph for that—but in the briefest of forms I strive to bring a character, a time, and a place to life. It's as if someone has lit a candle inside my skull, and the images take shape like hot wax melting deep into the valleys, arroyos, and unknown caves of my brain. What these photos capture, what they depict, burns: the fire of memory.

I continue to move back and forth from a photograph to my writing, closely looking at the photo, quickly composing a snapshot that's pinned down with words I write without hesitation. There at the library table I begin writing the draft of what I'll one day publish as "Avenue of the Americas, circa 1952." I'll carry the draft around for years, working—digging, sifting, recombining, rearranging—the words again and again with the hope of letting them say: *remember this flame.*

AVENUE OF THE AMERICAS, CIRCA 1952

Standing against a wall, an immaculate white cloth draped over a tray, Changó, nine years old, stands military straight, a jagged straw hat cocked on his head, a tattered shirt smudged with dirt reaching just below his elbows. Coloring the pristine white cloth, three green-and-red mangoes, a pair of cow shanks and hooves, a pig's foot, a chopped-up ox tail, the translucent bones clean and vivid with blood, with the succulent morsels found there. These butcher scraps, this reprise from his sore hands in a field holding a machete. This white cloth dazzling against his dirty clothes, his eyes. Changó must've washed it each night in a clear running stream he heard singing of shells and stars on its shapely voyage to the sea.

People pass, anticipating the briefest gestures of a hand in a pocket, the click of a gold clasp on a purse, he's ready for this woman who stops to buy a piece for stew. A few coins shimmer on the cloth next to a pale goat's tongue.

For a moment, beyond his memory of fields—picking thorny pineapples outside Arecibo, harvesting coffee in the mountains of Lares, cutting cane in the low fields of Añasco, selling mangoes in a plaza in the dusk—my father follows the blue cobblestones of the avenue, catches the fading sunlight still bright on the facade of a lime green house. Within the undulating grillwork of a black balcony, in those delicately rendered cast-iron vines of roses and leaves, seashells and stars, he gazes from within himself at a young boy who sees without the sting of sweat in his eyes.

Forever it's a quiet afternoon of soft and clean hands in the library. The table is a bright golden pine. I turn a glossy page to come upon a photograph of a boy standing on a street corner selling fruit. A few mangoes, a papaya, a trio of oranges with short stems and leaves—all displayed on a small table that's draped in a white cloth. The boy's straw hat and shirt stained with dirt and sweat. Time shatters like a rum bottle against a wall, and with those fragments I begin to piece together my father's story. There, carefully picking up the shards, the photograph helps me to remember my father's working childhood. But there are so many fragments the words begin to crowd the page and the gaps and silences grow wider, deeper. I hear within them that I can't forget the boy who asked for help. Even if these stories don't seem connected, are not smooth, correct, or telling an expected story, I might still bring them together, compose them into their own special song.

People ask, *Is that you?* As if I've taken this photo from an album. I smile, shake my head. I focus on the edges, the people in the dark doorways, the movement and stillness, the rubble and dirt piled in a mound at the end of the road. The sepia shadows. I imagine a Caribbean island, these gray, sun-bleached and sea-torn buildings part of a sugar mill, and the wake of a hurricane everywhere the eye touches. People all alone, adrift in a disaster they can't control. The barefoot boy walks away from a day's work, or he's on his way to find work, or there's nothing else to do but walk. There's only *un andadura*.

I found the photograph inside a shoebox. After visiting Thomas Wolfe's boyhood home, I decided to check out an antique shop and started sifting through the postcards and photos piled on top of a glass jewelry case. My heart skipped, rose into my throat. The photo spoke to me with an urgent mystery. I bought it for a dollar, and for the last twenty years it has been a part of my life. And even though it became the cover for a collection of stories, I'm still trying to piece together its story. The boy walks toward me. Where's he going? Like an open face, like open arms, like a long-lost friend or relative, he continues to walk toward me. He stops. He offers *un abrazo fuerte.*

Working Days

"*I've never lived as you do, but I know what you mean. When the night is dark—why, the stars are sharp-pointed, and there's quiet. Why, you rise up and up! Every pointed star gets driven into your body. It's like that. Hot and sharp and—lovely.*"

—JOHN STEINBECK, "THE CHRYSANTHEMUMS"

One of my favorite books is Jackson L. Benson's *The True Adventures of John Steinbeck*. Even at more than one thousand pages, I knew once I finished reading it that I was receiving only a glimpse into Steinbeck's story. Still, I felt the passion and dedication he had for his art and life, how he continually changed to become a better writer, how in each book he tried to write something he had never attempted before, and thus found himself in a place where "it was like starting all over again." In September 1948, struggling with the pain of divorce, he returns to California to live in a small house in Pacific Grove on Eleventh Street. Benson writes, "It seemed to be John's 'corduroy period,' in that he wore corduroy pants, corduroy shirts, and had a corduroy jacket. When [George] Robinson commented on this, John said, 'I love the feel of it—it's not snob material.'"

Here I am in this photograph, roughly seven years after Steinbeck's death and some forty years before I write these words, dressed in a smooth pale blue corduroy western suit. I remember it was a big purchase, some twenty dollars, just for me to wear on the plane to Puerto Rico. I've already put on more weight (and for the next three decades I'll struggle with obesity, high blood pressure, diabetes). There's a long stain near the bottom of the shirt stretched over my stomach, probably from dribbling cane or mango or orange juice when I bite into the ripe fruits. You can see my favorite mountains in the background, the sky dark on the edge from a storm rising over the Caribbean. Whenever a horse or ox was needed to work in a distant field, the truck I am standing on transported the animal, the steel pipes and rope and board holding the beast of burden tall and still like a statue floating down the road. *En General* are the only words I can read along the truck's back fender (perhaps it reads *Servecio En General*). On the edge of the fender and along my legs are the shadows of palms. The ox's hooves ring against wood and steel as he's herded up into the back of the truck over two wide planks. Standing on the side, I raise my hand toward his neck, one last smooth palm on the top of his head—he turns in a quick jerk, his head slamming against the steel pipe, his horns just missing my pulled-back arm. The old farmer hits the ox's haunches with his straw hat, *suave, chico, suave*, he yells, and yanks hard on his tail. The muscles in his shoulders go rigid, like cement, his eyes big and the whites filled with lightning-like red, his mouth and tongue wet with saliva. It's as if he blames me for taking him away on this truck, as if I am the god who sets his working days in motion. I want to tell him I'm sorry, tell him he'll be back, it will all be okay, soon he'll stand in his field. I hold the pipe for a moment, look deep into his eyes, see the swaying cane reflected within, feel the palm shadows on my legs.

I dream this over and over. The end is always same: I let go, drop down on the road, and my father hands me my camera.

Years later I was in Chico, California, at a bookstore when I found Steinbeck's biography looking hardly used and marked down to $12.50. They were having a 50 percent off sale, and for $6.25 I couldn't pass it up. The night before I had given a reading at the university, and the chair of the English Department had spoken with eloquence about how my characters and stories reminded him of Filipinos working in the fields, and of the shared experiences and stories in the literature.

Outside Big Sur, on Highway 1, I had passed a lettuce field on a thin strip of land shrouded in the early morning fog, the workers bent over and steadily picking dressed in gray or dirty white shirts and gloves and hats, their heads wrapped in cloth so I couldn't make out their faces, the Pacific roaring in endless waves.

I trembled inside for what the professor said, felt sharp points like horns spreading up into my ribs, across my shoulders, down my arms, and into my hands; both astonished and afraid of who I'd become, how I still carried that boy inside and yet had discovered a man who could write his way into another life, across regions, even into distant countries. I wasn't special, there wasn't anything unique about what I did, nor was I very smart. I just stared for a long time at ordinary things, held within me images that I let swirl and swirl through my memory and imagination until they became a deep river. When I sat down to write they welled up in my mind, I tried to feel and see through them, and they helped me to write down the words.

It was an experience akin to what Elisa—in "The Chrysanthe-mums"—calls *planting hands*:

"Well, I can only tell you what it feels like. It's when you're picking off the buds you don't want. Everything goes right down into your fingertips. You watch your fingers work. They do it themselves. You can feel how it is. They pick and pick the buds. They never make a mistake. They're with the plant. Do you see? Your fingers and the plant. You can feel that, right up your arm. They know. They never make a mistake. You can feel it. When you're like that you can't do anything wrong. Do you see that? Can you understand that?"

I took the biography home, and for the next year I read only Steinbeck. I had read some of his stories before, and I had read *The Grapes of Wrath* in a literature course, but Steinbeck wasn't a writer many esteemed. I was reading him alone, and there were so many stories for me to get to know. It was a revelation to follow his life and writings, to explore the depths of his curiosity and art, his focus on craft and process, his engagement with history and society. And when I encountered *Working Days: The Journals of The Grapes of Wrath* and *Journal of a Novel: The East of Eden Letters*, I felt once again the beautiful mystery of writing. It was as if Steinbeck was speaking over the years solely to me, helping me to realize that my search for a writing life was not in vain. They were words offered from a friend. I was born again, and I discovered a new childhood. I looked back and saw a progression of houses and apartments, empty rooms, a broken table, a cup without a handle, a bottle of rum lying on the floor; a train steaming on the tracks, a river rippling with gold currents, a trout rising into a silver-and-white waterfall, and a truck loaded with broken pieces of steel and wrinkled aluminum crossing a bridge in the dusk; palms swaying in the breeze, a hand gripping a machete glinting with sun, thick puffy clouds passing over red and yellow and white and lime boats drifting in a blue-green sea, and a Paso Fino horse trotting across a burned field; men leaning against a brick wall at first light, walking in a dusty lane with burlap sacks hanging over their shoulders, standing at the end of an assembly line, lifting a box in unison and dropping it with hard satisfaction on a pallet.

Steinbeck helped me to see the world anew, his pages were brilliantly colored windows into my life, and he made me look with wonder through the fenestra of memory. There was much I might save—no, bring to life, honor and make art from—if I put in the work and days, one after the other, *poco a poco*, my small paragraphs creating a world of peoples, regions, and stories alive on the page.

All I needed was a cheap notebook and a pencil. (And the aloneness I was gifted as a child: sent away on a plane, asleep in a closet, wandering through a plaza at night, following a stream making its way to the sea . . .)

When I came across those lines about his return to Pacific Grove, it struck me that Steinbeck wasn't being made fun of but questioned for his choices, criticized because he was being nostalgic in returning to his childhood and youth, perhaps his memory of a California he wouldn't find again. He was giving up his *working days* for his "corduroy days." Yet I could see that he was trying to dip once again into his wellspring, and in his choice of material there was something underneath: the mysterious and sacred things he held close, the things he loved, the peoples and places and words he had to write.

> Elisa watched them for a moment and then went back to her work. She was thirty-five. Her face was lean and strong and her eyes were clear as water. Her figure looked blocked and heavy in her gardening costume, a man's black hat pulled low down over her eyes, clodhopper shoes, a figured print dress almost completely covered by a big corduroy apron with four big pockets to hold the snips, the trowel and scratcher, the seeds and the knife she worked with. She wore heavy leather gloves to protect her hands while she worked.

I remember the softness of my suit, how smooth and clean and nice for a young boy who followed its blue in the sky and the sea. I loved the feel of it just as much as the red dust along the ox's hooves and ankles, an ochre-throated hummingbird hovering over the tip of my finger, and the greens of the swaying palms. These were colors one need not be rich to buy. They weren't, in fact, for sale. I held them without a fifty-cent piece in my palm—nor even a nickel inside the pocket of my corduroy suit.

—For Rob Davidson

Nights in the Gardens of Spain

Calle de Zapatos was a euphemism for a street in Madrid where, as the name suggests, you'd find many shoe stores. Farther from the bustle of the city center, however, the *calle* became almost parklike with small squares, trees, and benches off to the side, quiet places to take a rest and watch the world go by. There was also a small aluminum storefront, not much bigger than the entrance to a thin alleyway or a kiosk outside a bull ring, that I'd walk to for a snack in that twilight time after the day's siesta. The shop had a bar facing the street, barrels and taps behind it, the whole shallow space maybe six feet by three, and for a euro and a half I was given a large plastic cup of *cidré* and an *empanada* of tuna in a rich tomato sauce. I would stand at the bar or walk a few yards away and sit on a bench to enjoy my snack. I opened my copy of *The Marks of Birth*, and in between sips and bites I read a few paragraphs. That first glass of cider was cold and bubbly, sharp with something like iron and the crisp bite of sweet apples and fermentation. I often ordered a second glass and then walked down Calle de Zapatos farther away from the city center to some new plaza. I'd find a bench or chair. By the time I was halfway through that second glass of cider I'd be lightheaded—the cream- and mango-painted buildings, the iron scrollwork of the balconies, the flowering maroon-and-purple bougainvillea, the burnt red cobblestones shiny with the bluing light of the evening sky, a pattern of light, color, shadow, and smell thrumming in my chest. The last few sips of *cidré* memory.

Creaking ladders, shaking boughs, the tumbling thud of apples dropping into a wooden box, my parents back to work picking apples. A festival—apple pies, cider, apple cake, dried apples, the puckered cheeks of dolls in calico dresses whose faces were carved from apples—standing on a makeshift stage of plywood, the announcer yelling go, and with an apple in my palm, a knife in the other, I try to peel the longest apple skin anyone has ever seen. A long red dirt road glistening in the sun. Sugar cane swaying, a green mountain surrounded by blue, and at my feet gold-and-red mangoes like apples in Michigan.

Those last sips, the final scents and flavors bringing me to my old white ox sweating in a field of cane. Memory, always memory, taking me to where it must go, like a stream dammed for a moment, growing in strength, turning a mill, and finding its way to become what it must always become.

*
**

The fountain splashed little silver drops along its stone rim. African winds had brought the feeling of summer, the spring sky an endless blue tinted with the sun's gold warmth. There were tables displaying pottery, many *cazuela* pots and dishes, utensils, baskets, and crafts made on *fincas* outside Madrid. It was a festival for el Dia de San Isidro, the patron saint of farmers. Beyond the vendors a handful of people were strolling in the plaza. A quiet Sunday afternoon. The *cazuelas* were of the earth, red and brown with glints of mica, and smooth around the edges and inside. I had read that to cure a pot you cut the top off a head of garlic, rub it all along the bottom, fill the pot with water and vinegar, almost to the top, and then bring it to a slow boil. The *cazuelas* seemed indestructible and I made a mental note that before I left Spain I'd buy one to take into the rest of my life.

My bag was full with books, papers, a bottle of wine. I slipped the strap over my head, rested it on the ground. I took off my jacket, wiped my brow, and lifted the bag back to my shoulder. I tried to fold my coat over the top, the extra weight cutting the strap into my neck, and I jerked back and looked up into the sky, dizzy in the heat. I readjusted the strap and folded the coat over the crook of my arm. *Isidro, Isidre, Isodore*—the names quickly mixed together, and I heard *sidra*, and then *cidré. Cider. Sikera.* I let the names echo in my mind—*yes, I want you*—and just before they were all lost, I found that I was once again in that region I did not have a language to exist in (Jack Kerouac: "I never had a language of my own"). The names mixed, my head like a *cazuela* trying to hold and calm the rolling and bubbling languages, the words casseroling in my inner ear ("I've mixed them all in my head," Kerouac again). Then I held Isidro the farm laborer in my mind, stilled him for a moment, and watched as he was visited by angels, dropped his hoe, red dust powdering his ankles, the edges of his tattered smock. The angels swept him up in a flurry, flew into the sky and became a puffy cloud floating over the brown fields. San Isidro, the holy farmer, floating far and wide, crossing the sea to become Johnny Appleseed with his tin pot hat and sack of seeds tramping across America to bring countless orchards to life. And I had this inkling that maybe it didn't matter where I stood, where I lived, where I called home. What was more essential was that names had sounds I had to hear in Spanish and English, sounds I had to hear traveling between languages, traveling from here to there, soft sounds rolling together like the splashing fountain, calling me to follow them into regions of desire, memory, and story. Song. Seeds flung into the air.

*
**

The poet and his partner drove down never-ending roads, took countless twists and turns, and turned onto a long gravel road, just past a white clapboard church, and followed it to where it ended and the woods began. There was a house, a garage, an outbuilding— all the same design and wood, a shiny and smooth brown tinted with ochre. The outbuilding was a shop that sold various balsam products—balsam spray, small bags of balsam, and different-size balsam pillows covered with scenes of the North Country, each one redolent of its filling, a Maine woods on a bright summer day, a breeze.

I wandered away from the shop down the sloping yard to the gurgling stream I heard through the trees. The water was swift, silver pocked, with big black rocks and boulders, and no other sounds save the rushing water. Upstream there was an old crumbling wall of stone, the outline of a dam still visible in the leftover stones, the water spilling over its lip in a curtain of pewter. Chickadees hopped in the trees. I followed the stream with my eyes, back toward where we turned off the road, and looked up through a break in the trees: the thick blue sky, a solitary cloud approaching the edge of a green mountain.

When I returned to the shop, I asked about the wall. There had once been a mill, the owner told me, and pointed to the grindstone displayed on a large wooden pedestal just outside the door. When the folks from the university came down, they found the remnants of barrels and oxen shoes some two hundred years old.

I stepped to the door, looked back through the trees, listened for the stream.

There had once been an apple orchard here. Barrels made from the trees. Oxen lumbering through the woods pulling logs or a wagon. Apples stuffed into barrels, the oxen delivering them to the river, where they'd ship down to the coast and the waiting schooners, soon departing from the new world to the old.

In his book of poems he had inscribed:

For Fred–

> *May you find "home" in these pages. In the words of Elizabeth Bishop:*
> *"Should we have thought of here and stopped at home, wherever that might*
> *be"–*

I knew the lines from "Questions of Travel" well, remembered
them a bit differently, but the force of possibility was still there as I
brought together the two versions in my memory:

> Continent, city, country, society:
> The choice is never wide and never free.
> And here, or there . . . No. Should we have stayed at home,
> wherever that may be?

I opened the door, walked back through the trees to the stream,
and stood by the mill.

Soon I would have to go back. I'd stop in the shop for a moment
and buy at least two of the smaller pillows, hand size, one for my
son and the other for my writing table so I can breathe deeply the
memory of balsam.

I walked along the stream, listening to water slip past, around,
and over rocks. I loved the warmth of the sun on my arms and
face, the green bleeding through the dead leaves and branches and
needles, and the sounds of the stream. I followed the ground—no,
it was impossible to find an ox's shoes, but I felt myself searching
for bits of the past. Through the trees, past patches of shade, the
stream glittered.

*
**

Whenever I walked toward my apartment in Lavapíes, I felt as if I were descending a hill toward a river or sea. I never carried a map, stood at countless corners, looked down one alley or *calle*, down another, wondering which way to go. Often I simply looked between buildings for a square of blue twilight and took the *calle* that might lead that way. But spring wasn't always warm, and with the return of cold there came fog, a wide gray wave following the twisting, tight curves of a street and pushing me downhill into a plaza. Every evening had its own special itinerary, its unique discoveries—the fog blooming white against the red, green, and yellow neon *de una taberna*. I was lost in a new barrio. Madrid a vast, complicated citadel in the middle of the Castilian plain, and yet I was standing in the wet, cold fog of a port town. I felt I could smell the sea.

I always seemed to find an immigrant bar on these walks, the zinc a bit dull, the beer warm and skunky, the neon too bright, and the men's clothes still dusty and stained from the day's work, their features more mestizo or Asian than a *madrileño* businessman's. Intoxicated by the street, the light and the shadows, the smells and the sounds, *cidré* and brandy, and the rhythms of spoken Spanish, I stood at the bar. The fog filled the window, the men talked and laughed, and I tried to isolate the rays of neon mixing with cigarette smoke wafting over the bar and the fog drifting along the street. I touched my book bag on the stool. I ordered another *carajilla*.

In the mirror behind the bar was a man who had grown heavy in the shoulders and jaws, who couldn't make it through the day without glasses, his forehead lined and wrinkled. Who had I become? Who was I, really? Who cares? Why was it even important to ask the question? I so often hated to see my face in the mirror, the slight crook of my nose, the large brown mole, the thick hair I couldn't comb, the shy, dreamy eyes that would rather look at the ground. And equally I hated so much of my life, worried over my days, questioned what gave me the right to try to write. Teaching ignited that lost childhood self, his anxiety, and with that the hard, hot moments of punching my thighs and gut when the nausea rose from out of my stomach into my throat. My hands were soft, my tailbone and back tender from too much sitting. Day after day I would have to hide my quiet, tentative, solitary self to talk and perform for an hour, sometimes three—and sometimes I couldn't muster the character or mask to do it. Somedays it felt like my life had turned into a lie. (I belonged in a field, standing on an assembly line, drunk in some anonymous hotel on the shabby side of town, dead.)

My favorite part of the day became the night hours from 10:00 p.m. to 2:00 a.m., when I'd sit at my table, a circle of soft gold lamplight falling on a sheet of paper, the fragrance of wine or brandy my company, jazz playing softly in the background (or the music off and the wind softly swaying the chimes outside my window). I sat and remembered. I was no one, nothing, in those hours where I pushed consciousness away and let the other side of memory enter my brain. I often walked in the rumor of Epicurus's garden: *Stranger, here you will do well to tarry; here our highest good is pleasure.* I learned the possibilities of aloneness and how my melancholy needed this circle of light, the wind, the fragrances. The chance to welcome the stranger who might stand in my doorway and ask for forgiveness or shelter or redemption within the lonely walls of my temporary garden.

I finished my *carajilla*, my tongue searching out the brown sugar at the very bottom of the cup, the strong smell of brandy and coffee still thick in my nose, the back of my throat. I picked up my book bag, crossed the bar, and stepped into the fog.

I had traveled to Madrid to teach a graduate seminar in ethnic American literature. The university paid me generously, I was given a free apartment, the semester was short, and my seminar met for three hours on Tuesday evenings. The rest of the week was mine, and the great luxury of my days was sitting in a café or bar writing.

I had so much companionship; the novels and essays we read in the seminar seemed driven by compelling forces that fed directly into my writing: many ethnic American writers composed a kind of fictional biography of their parents, as if that generation held some secret or mystery one had to find the key for. Words revealed the marks of birth.

In his *In Praise of Shadows* Jun'ichirō Tanizaki writes,

> But we Orientals, as I have suggested before, create a kind of beauty of the shadows we have made in out-of-the-way places. There is an old song that says, "the brushwood we gather—stack it together, it makes a hut; pull it apart, a field once more." Such is our way of thinking—we find beauty not in the thing itself but in the patterns of shadows, the light and the darkness, that one thing against another creates.

When I look back on my nights in Madrid, I want to remember the light and the darkness, the patterns of shadows in those streets and taverns, in those moments when no one knew me and I was offered a chance to remember who I might have been. Memory became a form of dreaming. I couldn't always find beauty in memories, no matter how hard I tried to return to their origins. I discovered that only by selecting my memories, only by placing them side by side, only by placing myself next to my father (and those long-ago Puerto Rican men from childhood and the physical labor that stole their bodies, their sweat, their souls, and their names), only then might I create some strange pattern in which I might hear a story I could live with. A story I might live by.

But, alas, first I had to immobilize moments like this. I had to praise the moment's shadows.

I took a deep breath. Exhaled. Disgusted by that face in the mirror. I was also falling apart in Madrid. I had a handful of friends who were too far away, had no family I could share my secret with. Yes, back in the States I had a beautiful wife and my precious two-year-old son. But I had spent the last six years away from my wife, and in the two years of my son's life I was lucky to spend six or eight days out of the month with him, and I had to drive almost seven hundred miles on each trip. I walked more quickly, the loss and loneliness becoming too heavy. My wife and I had grown apart; she was driven by a career, by money and security, whereas nothing was certain in my life, and my bank account held barely enough to get by for a few weeks. All she wanted, besides security, was a child—no matter what happened to me, no matter what I did or became, I could at least give her a child. There was no way I could stop my terrible thoughts: *I'm not certain I want to be a father. I don't know how to be a father—or maybe I was never taught how to be one.* All I wanted, couldn't stop imagining, was to stay in Madrid. To make my life here in this utterly foreign yet familiar city. Stay on until the teaching ended, then take up meeting people in cafés and bars and teaching English through conversation, roaming the streets and finding something I might call a life. Sit. Drink *cidré*. Wash dishes in some out-of-the-way restaurant. Stroll in a garden. Watch the blue sky, the clouds, the wind in the trees, walk at night with the fog until I was lost forever. Or find where the shadows might take me.

I heard the poet call through the trees, *Freddie. Vamanos, hombre.*

The poet and I shared the same publisher, had a few mutual friends, but had never met in person. One night we were both in Washington, D.C., and over martinis talked the evening away as if we were continuing conversations we had started years ago. At one point I told him that I'd had a mental picture of his house. There were these images of a weathered, cedar-sided cabin; fir, pine, and birch trees; and he stood at the edge of his house, half in sunlight, half in tree shadows. I called these images a dream because, although they were mixed up with memory, I had no way to account for them. Did I see them in a magazine article? Had I written into existence such a place in my notebook? He seemed pleased, even a bit astonished by my description. He didn't know where those images existed, but it became suddenly a story we shared; there at the bar, in that moment, he believed my words, my dreams.

We laughed, talked more of life and writing. We shared a connection of having lived in Hartford, Connecticut, at different times. We knew each other only through our writings, but it was as if we were old friends, men who shared sensual details, strong clear images and memories, smells and tastes of lives that were miles away and yet so near, as they somehow survived deep inside our bodies. One thread of the conversation led to another, and he invited me to stay in his cabin for a month so I could continue writing. *A kind of residency, if you will, because my partner and I are thinking of offering the cabin to writers in the summer,* he said. *You could be the guinea pig.* I couldn't believe my luck, his generosity. He was bringing me, someone he didn't know from Adam, into his home.

I walked back to the store, and we left the balsam woods and drove down to the coast, where, after a long, twisting drive, we stopped in a small cove for dinner at a lobster pound. That night we stayed in a bed and breakfast, and I slept on an air mattress out in a small screened-in porch. The scent from the lilacs was heavenly, and though a storm woke me in the middle of the night, the cooling rain falling through the trees gave me one of the best nights of sleep I'd ever had.

We continued down the coast, the poet's partner driving with the top down, and when I looked over my shoulder, the poet was lying in the backseat, looking up into the sky, as he composed a poem on the back of an envelope with a red pen.

In his *Itinerary: An Intellectual Journey*, Octavio Paz writes,

> One afternoon, leaving the school at a run, I suddenly stopped; I felt
> I was at the center of the world. I raised my eyes and saw, between
> two clouds, an open blue sky that was indecipherable and infinite.
> I did not know what to say: I discovered enthusiasm, and, perhaps,
> poetry.

I let those words swirl in my mind, whirl out into the backseat and become one with the sunlight enveloping the poet, and like a wave the light returned to me: I was still but radiant in the moment as the wave pulsed through me. The moss-covered granite walls we passed, the thick green firs sparkling with beads of gold sunlight, the azure coves frothing white against the red and pink stones on the shore—they would stay with me until I discovered how they might help me to name the country I was traveling toward. Two puffy clouds drifted above the road, the yellow lines darkening, and I shivered when a momentary shadow fell over the car, my shoulders, my hands.

We eventually turned back to the mountains and drove home. Once I was back inside the cabin, my small balsam pillow on the edge of my table, I found there was still enough daylight to look out into the birch trees filling with the yellowed twilight and begin writing the very words someone might one day read on this page. (I will always be grateful for those writing days.)

I still had several weeks to write, I had found my way back, and I want to say that a simple moment like this, an elbow resting on the edge of the table, my chin resting in the palm of one hand, a pen in the other, I was beginning to write who I might become, even in the face of so much anxiety, uncertainty, and loss. The evening was already cooling, a slow bank of fog drifting down from the mountains and meeting the last yellow light sifting through the trees. It felt good to know that after being away for a month in the North Country, I wanted to return to my son.

For now I knew there was only one way home. And that was the country awaiting my arrival as I traveled across the page.

*
**

Up above the two tallest firs, in a patch of still blue sky, a small moon glows. In the fridge I have an unopened bottle of cider from Quebec. *Mis en bouteille au verger.* Cold, sweet, and tart, I write, crisp, *bottled in the orchard*, and place myself later in the night out on the deck, looking at the moon through the gauzy strips of fog still trying to cling to the earth, the trees, lifting the cider to my lips.

Calle de Santiago

Quickly, before it's lost, I must remember the other side of Madrid: Calle de Santiago. Real or imagined, remembered or misremembered, it was a long street that curved around and down from the Plaza Mayor. In my memory it's the name for all the cafés I sat in, my thick manuscript on the edge of an iron table, my notebook open in front of me, a pen in my hand, and on the other edge a *copa* of brandy and a *cortado*. When I looked up from my writing, still lost in the blue sky of Michigan, a cold spring wind blowing through a grove of birches so hard I could see the shredded bark on the trunks flickering white and black, I saw across the street, on the corner of a building, the *azulejos* and the name Calle de Santiago.

In Madrid I worked day and night rewriting and reinventing a novel I had been working on for more than ten years (I wrote four different books, threw each away, and now felt I was finally on the right path, *un andadura*). I wore a dark blue fleece against the chill spring air, a few pens zipped in its chest pocket, and with *copa* after *copa* of coffee and brandy I wrote until the air became too cold, my hand no longer following the images burning in my mind. That spring was almost too fertile as I pushed myself toward exhaustion. I found myself dreaming and writing a second book alongside my novel, and the title seemed to arise out of nowhere, from some place deep within, and then I recognized it as an old jazz standard: "Close as Pages in a Book." I had understood without any doubt that I was now free of my father—physically, geographically, economically. I had been irrevocably changed by my education and the hundreds of books I had read, and I had traveled to jobs and places he would've never dreamed. I thought I was utterly alone, but I still struggled to quiet the voices and languages, the men like my father who continued to crowd their way into the library of my mind. I began to understand that I was living my life *close as pages in a book*, as every page I read added to, changed, and confirmed my life. And yet as the books accumulated within my psychic library, I found the pages always returned me to my father's work, drink, and silence. His life was written in between the lines of the pages I read, lightly composed in the margins, and often with a rage no page could ever contain. Even if each page I read confirmed my father's absence from a life of the mind, from the scenes and places and stories, each still drew me closer to him, drew me deeper into the memories and mysteries of his life. Each page I encountered was a mirror, and in its reflection I recognized that none of my reading mattered unless I acknowledged what was missing, what was silent, who was lost, the outlines of faces I could not read in the words, faces blurred in the mirror.

I was reading my life in so many of the pages I read. I wrote quickly and passionately an essay draft on the first contemporary novel I had read, which I found at a library book sale, Kevin McIll-voy's *The Fifth Station*, and focused on how the novel's depiction of character and work and class and place and family helped me to see so much of the dignity and power of my own poor working life. I put together pages of notes on Leslie Marmon Silko's *Ceremony*, which I thought of as the great twentieth-century work of art, and how in it I encountered *arroyo* for the first time in a book, and how an arroyo became both the central scene and metaphor for the novel and its beautiful exploration of witchery and healing. (I counted my name more than one hundred times in Silko's pages.) I knew that I had to write something on *The Sun Also Rises*, and I had to account for how Jean Rhys, Ernest J. Gaines, and V. S. Naipaul influenced my writing. Many take literacy for granted, I thought, but I had to praise and honor its gifts.

Every year, usually in the middle of winter, when I suffered the darkest days of depression, I turn to Jim Harrison's *Farmer* and understand once again that his poetic prose is a part of my lyricism. And even though I know I must work, I must survive, there is much more I want from life. I ponder these words by Harrison season after winter season (and know I must claim them):

> But to the truly gifted one like Samuel or John Keats, knowledge was as real as a leaf or a mud puddle. They found music to dance to in the most ordinary things. They did not live with distant thoughts of the ocean, or endure countless monotonous days in order to hunt and fish or simply read about hunting and fishing and the Indian and Caribbean and Arctic Oceans. Joseph believed that Keats and Whitman and young Samuel somehow lived in the purest reaches of their imaginations and there was a beauty in it that wasn't found in the preoccupations of others; say making a living which turned out to be nothing other than what comes simply and directly to most animals.

When you are first trying to write there are so many false starts you wonder how anything is ever written. When you begin imagining writing that is longer than, say, a poem, a story, or a brief essay (it's not yet a book and yet you feel it will take some considerable words to discover its shape), you often create false starts. These beginnings are the well-lit doorways needed to enter the rooms you must write. You approach these false starts with great seriousness because they are all you have. Over time, though, after much writing and invention, the writing offers its own urgent energy and itinerary, and your original beginnings seem untrue to the emerging life of the book. Still, these false starts are essential for everything that exists on the page. They are deep inside the book you eventually compose—like an invisible river flowing through your words. Or: they set in motion *un andadura*.

This is all very much as Patrick Modiano expresses in his novel *So You Don't Get Lost in the Neighborhood.* He has a character, Darange, a novelist himself, who can't find the first two chapters from his first novel. They were chapters that had to be written for the novel to exist, and yet Darange discovers that they had no place in the novel if it were to have a life of its own. Modriano writes of these *real losses* and *imaginary gains* in this way:

> And so he started all over again from the beginning with the painful sense that he was correcting a false start. And yet the only memories he retained of this first novel were the two chapters he had discarded that served as underpinning for everything else, or rather as scaffolding you remove, once the book is finished.

Trying to write *Close as Pages in a Book* at that moment in my life was a false start. I will always remember those pages, the books—the *scaffolding*—that gave me a new, wondrous life. Those years carried me into the future, and as I remember the dark mystery of those many books, those passionate moments of reading, of beginning a transition to a new country, I can't see how it could have been any other way.

"If I were asked to name the chief event in my life," Jorge Luis Borges writes, "I should say my father's library. In fact, sometimes I think I have never strayed outside that library" ("An Autobiographical Essay"). Regardless of the many books I had read, I realized that my father's book is the central event of my life—even if it's a book made up of fragmented, scattered, and thrown-away pages, many of which I have never read. He let them disintegrate in some ditch on the side of a road, in fields, floating in some long-forgotten sea. Yet I've never seemed to find my way outside his pages. There is no other choice: I must live my life *close as pages in a book.*

As I worked on my novel I continued to remember the time when my father took me to Puerto Rico. We stayed in my grandparents' house, and after a few days he disappeared. I spent most of my days with my grandmother, my Abuela. I returned to one of the first things I tried to write—that sudden, inexplicable memory of Abuela in her kitchen, so vivid and alive, as if I was a boy once again walking down her gray cement hallway, the blue of the mosquito net I had slept under becoming all the more colorful as I stepped into the bright smells and colors of her kitchen. Every time I remembered Abuela words became brand new. Since the fifth grade I had lived in Michigan and struggled to fit in, had trouble with learning and had no way to express, let alone understand, the pain and shame of watching my father fall apart through his drinking. There was so much I had to suppress and silence, I was as shipwrecked as he, and even if we were on the same island, we had washed up on distant shores. And what never washed up between us was Spanish, and thus our memories of Puerto Rico never reached us, were never shared. When I look back now at how I made it through the days, it saddens me to understand those years were only about surviving—surviving work, his drinking, the lack of money, the emotional weight of accepting the rage, the yelling, his hand or a fist, the anxious sea deep in my stomach and mind, the taste of blood in my mouth. Childhood was a home where imagination could not exist. I had no reason to remember my grandmother.

In the end, it's a silly memory, too private, too fragmented, and I'm exhausted by how all these memories return unexpectedly. That time with my father seems nevertheless eternal. A gift of my childhood that I'll never lose.

My parents' first house cost $30,000 (perhaps even less). I'm sure it was a fortune to them, even if it wasn't the best house to buy. It needed much work and was directly across the street from the Puerto Rican House. There I am in the backyard, a late-spring day, ready for summer to begin, and I've been obsessed with fishing. My father wants to paint the house bright lime green, too gaudy for Michigan. My mother asks him to drive us north to where there's a trout pond. He takes us, I catch ten or twelve beautiful rainbow trout, one after the other, in less than thirty minutes. We take them to the small shed for weighing and payment, and the trout are stacked in a clear plastic bag, placed on the scale, and their weight costs a little over twenty dollars. Another fortune they probably can't afford. Back home, in the backyard, my mother has brought out her silver-and-black pocket camera. My father is taking pictures of me holding the trout, and in the last one I try to step in behind my mother and hold the trout at her side, as if she were holding them. She screams, cannot take the closeness of those dead fish, and when she steps away, my father throws the camera at me; it strikes my stomach, hits the ground, and pops open exposing the film. No one says a word. The rage in his face turns his eyes black. His hands tremble at his sides. He's been drying out again, his chambray shirt wet with sweat, the sleeves rolled tight against his bulging forearms, the purple veins in his hands like thick rope. He has lost weight, and as he grinds his teeth his cheeks sink in and his jaw looks hard as an anvil. He walks over to the ladder, climbs it, and begins scraping old paint off the house. I've ruined another day, and I think if only he would yell at me, punch me, tell me to pick up a scraper or a wire brush and help him, then maybe he could paint the house faster. The rainbow trout have lost their color, are turning stiff, their skin filling with dark shadows.

There I was in Spain trying to leave my past behind when on every *calle* I saw my father walking in a crowd, sitting at a café table in an elegant blue shirt, heard Abuela's voice from some iron balcony yelling—*Freddie, Freddie, don't forget to buy bread.* That past shaped my novel, and I placed a character in the Plaza Santa Ana sitting in a tavern, looking at the people walking by, and deciding:

> I felt I had no choice: I needed to perfect my memory of Abuela. Once the words and pictures—the word-pictures—were just right, I'd tell my father about that time, I'd discover a way to say—to name— what needed to be said between us.
>
> It seemed like I had nowhere to turn. Sometimes, my life had its most immediate meaning when I saw it close as pages in a book.

Whatever dreams I had for that book are lost. I can't find the words for what I was so passionate about, can't remember what I hoped to write. Words I no longer have any connections with. Words of some lost self. Who cares what books changed anyone's life? Who would the books of my life speak to? Who out there wants to live his or her life close as pages in a book?

I'm not sure I fully understand what happened to all those passions. All I felt was that I'd never amount to anything writing that book. I wasn't very interesting, my life mattered to no one, and anything I wrote needed to be about someone or something other than me—I had to live in a fictional world in order to dream a better life. I was fond of paraphrasing Robert Kroetsch in that maybe *I was writing an autobiography in which I didn't appear.* And it was just as good to listen to John Keats say in his letters, "I feel assured I should write from the mere yearning and fondness I have for the Beautiful even if my night's labours should be burnt every morning and no eye ever shine upon them. But even now I am perhaps not speaking from myself; but from some character in whose soul I now live." There were souls I still needed to live in. By listening to them, by recognizing their voices, maybe, maybe only then, I might become a writer. Every apartment and house my father moved us to, every man he introduced me to, every night he took me out drinking with him—the person I was might be found back there in those apartments and houses, in those cars and bars, in those fields and factories, if I discovered how to listen to and write them with a yearning and fondness for the beautiful.

"Do what you most want to do, whether or not it is of any value to anyone else," M. F. K. Fisher writes. Over time I've taken the best I can from my father: his passion for drink, travel, work. A grand life in many ways, even if many will dismiss him as small, minor, better forgotten. If he had these words, in Spanish or English, I can hear him say, *Write your heart out. Write what you most want to write.* He might sound like Harry Crews, "I have found nothing in this life that can match the feeling of writing something I'm proud of." Then, suddenly, out of the thin air, he'd have his machete, hammer, or knife in his hands. He'd point it at me. *Don't worry too much about anyone else,* he'd say, *but don't make too much of it.*

How might I thank him for that? *Thank you, Santiago. Thank you, Papi.* That would have to be enough. Then I'd have to become silent because if I said any more it might become too painful. For I'd have to tell him how sad it is to write your heart out, how blue—*cómo azul*—the words are because in English there's this rich, particular life in another language I'll never be able to fully share. And I'd have to tell him that when I sat in a café on the corner of Calle de Santiago, I wrote without memory. All I wanted was the hunger for the words

that were just in front of me. So I'm not sure I ever placed any significance on my being there. I'm not even sure I took a moment to
understand how lucky I was to write on a street that held my father's
name. Or maybe it's better to remember the green palms, their
shadows tiger-striping the kitchen, the green breadfruits thudding
against the red dirt, the red-and-green mangoes swaying with the
breeze, the green limes in the middle of the table in a blue bowl, and
how a red-throated hummingbird zoomed in and out of the kitchen
through an open window. That is always true, and because I write
it down next to the cheap color my father chose to paint his house,
some form of lime green like blue in green, it makes it all the more
true. That takes me closer to the Santiago I'd give anything to find
sitting at a table.

White shirt, black pants, a thin black tie, and a white cloth draped
over her forearm. Her skin was a lovely smooth brown tinted with
cinnamon. She set a glass of brandy and a plate mounded high with
fried calamari surrounded by wedges of lemon on my table. *Thank
you.* I moved my manuscript closer to the edge, closed my notebook.
She asked if I was from California. *No. Why do you ask? A lot people
from California visit Madrid, and you look like you might be.* She asked
what I was working on. *Una novela,* a short novel set in Michigan
and Puerto Rico, and something like recognition flashed in her eyes.
I told her some of the story, and how good it was to be here with
voices and words and images appearing every day anew. Sometimes
I don't know where I'm from. She said that she was from Puerto
Rico, and her mother moved to Madrid when she was very young.
I haven't seen my family back there again. My mother never stayed
in touch. She looked at my steaming plate. She wished me luck with
my writing and my visit.

I ate my crispy calamari with the lemon squeezed over it. I reread and edited a handful of manuscript pages as I ate. Cool air drifted down the road like a wave from the sea—wet, cold, and thick gray as if it were laced with the salt I tasted in the calamari. Fog followed behind and I couldn't see across the street, only a few gray stones breaking through every so often. I opened my notebook and wrote a few paragraphs about a cool sunny afternoon when my two characters—Magdalene and Ernest—had lunch on a bluff, trying to capture how the battered and fried softshell crabs crunched and tasted and how cool white wine washed the taste away for a moment and then all the flavors bloomed in their mouths as they looked down on the bright azure of the freshwater sea, Lake Michigan. The waves hit the stone shore in white rollers, and the wind on the bluff was turning colder. I started to shiver and my fingers felt wet, were beginning to go numb. The quarter glass of brandy warmed me as I gulped it down, and when it hit the calamari deep in the pocket of my stomach my midsection was filled with fire. I packed my book bag.

I can't remember all that she said. I clearly see in my imagination— her hair, the color of her skin and her face, even down to her eyes the color of a long *finca* road outside Mocha and how under her left one, just on the edge of her cheekbone, there was a small scar, as if a pinch of her skin had been stripped away. Maybe she had never said anything about Puerto Rico. Maybe she is only one of many Puerto Rican women I've met who have never known their fathers, who without any bitterness lived far from places they couldn't return to. She was beautiful, elegant as she glided between the outside tables, and how could I forget that she took the time from carrying heavy trays loaded with glasses and plates, wiping down tables, sweeping the café patio as spotless as her white shirt, to stop and talk with me.

*
**

Somewhere the scholar Gustavo Pérez Firmat suggests that writers like me are composing a love letter to the Spanish language, and what is so strange in this writing, he says, is that the letter is written in English. That may be so. All I know is that the paragraphs I've been composing may, in the end, only add up to a fragmented love letter to my father. A stuttering letter to say all those things we were never able to say. And language? I'm not sure there is only one I love, and I know I cannot give my heart fully to English because it is a language I'll never own.

My father's gesture: he would extend his left arm stiffly at an angle above his waist, his index and middle finger pointing from his hand, and his right hand would become a machete and he would cut across his left arm just at the elbow or in the middle of his bicep, depending on the situation. The gesture was a version of his "great fever"; he made it when he was trying to describe something that was rich, tasty, even beautiful. I have always imagined it's a gesture he learned cutting cane: the more precise and perfect your cuts of cane, the easier the repetition of the work.

He had a way of turning the gesture against me in a critical and cutting way, never seeming to recognize the pain in his humor. If I had caught a large fish or done something I was proud of, he'd slowly close the distance between his open hands, his palms slowly moving toward each other, and ask, *How big?* His face serious, then a smile would begin as his machete hand cut below the elbow of his arm, and then right before he laughed he'd say, *Cut it back, cut it back a little, Freddie.* It didn't matter what the actual thing was because his words covered everything: *How big? Cut it back, cut it back a little, Freddie.* It was as if imagination couldn't be larger than reality. Reality was large enough—a distant snow-covered mountain—and held more wonder and weight than anything you could imagine. *Look around,* he might say. *Look right in front of your eyes. See my crooked hands, my worn shoes, my empty wallet?*

Less is more, he seemed to tell me in his silence. And I hold that as a special gift—*cut away as much as possible*. "In time we often become one with those we once failed to understand," Patti Smith once wrote. I loved his gesture—my father's love across time and languages—and catch a glimpse of it in my hand as I write these words.

I walked up Calle de Santiago through the fog toward the Plaza Santa Ana. I stopped outside the Café Central, leaned against the red façade as a lone trumpet headed out on an Aranjuez riff, a bright, high note pulling me toward the door, circling me, one *pase* after another, the note growing into other notes breathing tone and mood and space, each note like dust and sun and sweat swiftly passing through me. I eventually made my way up to the plaza and stopped in front of the statue of Federico Garcia Lorca. No one was sitting outside. The stone plaza gleamed as if it had rained. Couples walked in heavy coats, and the taverns looked warm with the inner gold light pouring from their windows meeting the strips of fog drifting through the empty outside tables and closed umbrellas. I touched the back of Lorca's hands, palms up holding a bird ready to take flight, its wings lifting over his hands. I don't recall ever walking down Calle de Santiago again, and I never returned to that café because the food and drinks were too expensive. And I was afraid of all the places that waitress took my heart. Instead I traveled deeper into Lavapies and found new taverns and cafés, new islands where I could sit and remember and imagine and dream. I needed these small places to discover how many birds might take flight from my hands, how many notes might soar from my words.

Sofrito

Abuela Monsa stands in her open kitchen. Steam rises with the song she hums. She dances and sways, moves back and forth from table to stove. Sunlight slants into the doorway, banana leaves shaking in the breeze, shadows falling in waves behind the sunlight and the leaves. A hummingbird flutters just above her shoulder, its purple throat turning silver against the color of Abuela's hair. She works between this morning's shadow and sun: she chops garlic, onions, cilantro, and tomatoes. She adds them to a pan of simmering rice.

I quietly step forward and watch her pour achiote oil into the pan, the rice turning a deep yellow. She lightly rubs the side of my cheek with the back of her hand, smiles, and then turns a small blue bowl over the pot sending a stream of glistening *gandules* trembling into the pan. She spoons coffee into a boiling pot of water, then adds a small cup of cream and a couple spoonfuls of sugar.

The kitchen: the doors wide open, windows without glass or screens, leaves and hummingbirds freely floating in, the sunlight filling the kitchen and tiger-striping the white-tiled floor.

Salt, black pepper, olive oil, and the sweet smell of mangoes ripening on the table. Such a wonderful silence: the lush shaking of leaves, fruit hitting the ground with a deep thud, Abuela's sandals scraping on the floor, her spoon striking the side of a silver pot.

Siéntate, Freddie.

She brings me a cup of coffee and a plate of yellow rice and *gandules* surrounded by slices of avocado and warm bread. This old woman, her flowered dress, her dark skin and silver hair. This first memory of my father's mother.

Some evenings the distance of memory overcomes me. Half a continent and a sea divide Abuela and me, and it was some forty years ago that I last stood in her kitchen watching her bring to reality colors (or weathers or airs) that seemed all the more important in each other's company. Now I take out a knife, a head of garlic, an onion, a small tomato, and a bunch of cilantro. I pour a small circle of olive oil into the middle of the cutting board. I rub the oil in a circle, slowly widening the circle until the board shines wetly. Imagining the circumference of the first circle, I place three generous pinches of sea salt and a handful of black pepper in the center. I crush them with the knife blade. Hit the blade once, twice, crush, crush, keeping the bits of salt and pepper in a black-and-white mound inside the circle. On the edge of this circle I chop up four garlic cloves, then add them to the circle. I crush and mince the garlic, salt, and pepper. Chop half an onion, six *ají dulce* peppers, add them to the circle, and mince again. I break the cilantro in my hands, my fingers wet, that earthy green scent releasing more than my memory: the slow, delicate mixing of the cilantro into this *sofrito* that'll shape the flavor and texture of a pot of rice I'll cook to honor Abuela.

I place the small tomato on the edge of the cutting board next to the knife.

I heat olive oil in a pot, scoop up the *sofrito* with my hands and drop it in. Steam rises, the *sofrito* singing of water and salt. I add two handfuls of rice. I stir the rice, letting the natural juices and water from the *sofrito* toast the rice. Steam lifts in wide almost shapeless arcs, my face is warm with the spicy fragrance of garlic and olive oil, salt and pepper. I have no achiote. I have no fresh *gandules*. I open and drain a can of pigeon peas, rinse them, let them tumble into the pot. Adding a handful of inexpensive saffron from Thailand, I pray that this time the rice will turn the deep orange-gold I always remember, that first bite coloring my mouth, leaving a long stain on its way to the deep pocket of my stomach. I pour in just enough water to cover the rice by about an eighth of an inch and stir. I turn to the tomato and slice it in half, into quarters, and then chop each quarter into small, angled wedges and cubes. I drop handfuls of dripping red into the pot, place a pat of butter directly in the center of the simmering rice slowly turning orange.

The lid can go on now; the flame turned to a low flickering blue. I simply leave the pot alone for thirty minutes.

Forty years away I wait for these minutes to cook down into this evening, that morning, this waiting. Tonight I'll sit here with a plate of yellow rice and pigeon peas and a glass of red wine. My twilight blues: a mixture of desire, memory, and ingredients that begin to make *sofrito*, an island, alive. A dog barks in the alleyway, then a chorus of dogs. My hands firm on the marble table, I look down on the alleyway, yellow leaves tumbling across uneven bricks in the twilight. The white Saab up on cinderblocks in the yard across the way floats in a sea of milk crates, soda bottles, and pieces of broken fence, rusty, twisted bicycles.

I haven't seen Charlie and Jill in a month, and I wonder how my three-year-old son has grown. I'm here with these paragraphs, too much failure, so much dream and memory, as I try to find beauty where there is only loss. Will he remember me the next time he sees me?

On the horizon the Basilica gathers the last of the sunlight, and here, in my private shipwreck, I feel the return to sea. The dogs pause all at once, either happy with their voices or exhausted. When I begin to eat the yellow rice and pigeon peas, I'll hear inside myself the crunch of salt, the tender peas uncovering themselves in each bite, my mouth suddenly more alive with flavors, colors. I'll briefly feel my loneliness and then the company of memory: An open doorway. A knife. A table. The briny burn of cheap Rioja. The pulsing purple throat of a hummingbird, Abuela Monsa's silver hair, and the humming of her song in the symphony of cooking, steam, and, in the distance, the caracoling sea.

Freight

When my son wasn't even a year old he suffered terribly from croup, a loud bark, ear infections. What I remember most: a wailing cry that scared me from sleep and how I held him against my shoulder, his fists balled up against my chest, whispering, *I've got you, my son, I've got you, my son, everything's okay.* We walked in a circle, a swaying dance across the wood floor, my voice a quiet song, my son responding with a creaky cough, a wail. And when he couldn't stop crying, I stepped out onto the cold fourth-floor porch, the moon overhead, the river moving silently below in that blue Milwaukee light. A freight train chugged out of the valley, hit the bridge like thunder, its lights spraying across the river as the engine pulled up to a row of warehouses. I still whispered softly, my son's fists against my heart. He breathed in the cold air, and his seal-like bark quieted, no longer crying, he slept in the moonlight alongside the rumble of freight.

There is a silver dish my father gave me. The lips of the dish are raised with bougainvillea vines and flowers, a vignette circling the miniature red scene in the middle: the words *Puerto Rico* writ large; an image of the island with a few major towns (Aguadilla, Mayagüez,

Ponce, Guayama, Río Piedras, San Juan, Bayamón, Arecibo); two bold roosters facing each other before a fight; the Atlantic Ocean on one side and the Caribbean Sea on the other, some tall palm and coconut trees growing from a small sandy beach, a sailboat cutting across thin waves below billowing clouds, and a lighthouse perched on the end of the scene. In the briefest of lines the artist spun to life a delicate handwriting forever in my blood. Images and objects from the shipwreck of childhood: the baby chickens we had in Hartford scalped by cats or city rats; the regal red rooster in our West Hartford backyard, a long blue line of string tied around his scaly yellow ankle, a path of cracked corn, and the underside of the back porch, his home; the black-and-white rabbits hunched in their wire cage, the purple clover I had gathered lying in a thick bunch in front of their twitching noses; the sharp click of maracas, salsa and rumba taking shape, the call-and-response of music and family as everyone danced between a few chairs and a coffee table in a warm, cramped apartment; the navy blue work uniform with a new strange name for my father, *Chuck*, in cursive over his heart. In Connecticut, Michigan, Illinois: the migrating tableau of a blackened silver pot brimming with yellow rice and pigeon peas, a plate of glistening *pastelles*, a dish of smothered chicken or rabbit (*pollo estofado, conejo estofado*), and a bottle of dark rum next to a half-full glass. And always the rhythm of the sea.

For some thirty years I've carried this dish around (perfect for holding loose change, propped against some books like a port-hole into forever and never, an arena of paperclips and fountain pen ink cartridges), and I don't remember when, where, or how it became mine. I assume my father gave it to me (as if the sil-ver etching might raise *Santiago* in memory, his name deeper and stronger behind *Chuck*). When I turn it over I find it was made in Japan and I have cracked it along the lip, a long scar around the edge of the rim.

When I moved to California with my eight-year-old son, I took him some fifteen hundred miles away from his mother. We had made the mistake of believing too much in an American Dream: we bought two houses, since we lived apart, and when the economy turned, our houses were "underwater," as they say. I went west for work and took our son so he could attend a good private school and because, when I was not teaching, I could take care of him. On the edge of the Pacific he was never sick. He learned to skateboard, found he wanted to grow his hair long, grew to love things Chinese and Japanese, and discovered that although he was not out on the prairie any longer, there are open spaces even in most densely populated places. He started singing in Spanish (*mañana, te quiero mañana*). He recognized the private power of reading. Like a wave that adds to and subtracts from a beach, I hope he and I will ride that year toward many tomorrows. I thought I gave him this dish in California. Memory was moving too fast, changing, and I needed something to contain it, even if it's cracked, the silver beginning to turn blue-green, almost gray. Maybe he declined it. Maybe he said I should keep it. Maybe I don't remember that I decided to wait, to let him grow some more, and then I could offer him this small life. Over time more stories will entwine themselves in these vines and flowers, and like that little lighthouse on the sea, I'll still be a keeper of memory, I'll still throw light on the freight of yesterday.

Pulsar Watches

My father was never a keeper of time. Working from the age of eight or nine, time might've been what he wished for the least, what he wanted to forget. I've closely watched how time silently patterned his body, his hands: he picks up a spade and strikes deep into the earth with one decisive slice; swings his gleaming machete through cane, each piece the exact length of his forearm; slides underneath a jacked-up car with a wrench, his knuckles streaked with grease under the bright lamp flooding his thin workspace; three or four months straight stumbling around the living room, knocking against a doorjamb, peeing in the corner of his bedroom, and then the days of moaning and crying, the violent tremors and shakes as he tries to raise a spoon or cup to his lips, seconds of sobriety filling his fingers with such caution, regret, and failure. His attention pulsing through his hands, his eyes, his tense shoulders—such elegance in the briefest of gestures—as I watched in drunk-time, sober-time, and work-time how there was no time for a watch.

The faces on these watches are the same—tan, starlike, rimmed in gold, always open—lying in my palms. Their hands don't turn, and one watch has a broken band, the small pin that holds it in place lost, a severed lone arm. I never like wearing a watch, and maybe do so only because many around me do. Part of one's fashion, a watch going well with a cuffed, pressed shirt. Years pass and I don't see my father. Then when we are together he'll gift me a timepiece. He seems to forget that he's given me a watch the time before, this new one not much different from the last, the same thick, brown band, sturdy like the harness on an ox pulling a cart stacked with cane. They'll work and last forever, take in sweat, dirt, rain, the Milky Way. Pulsar watches are not very expensive, although I sometimes look at where my father is headed in old age, and I imagine they might become part of a small fortune he'll need. I think he equates my trying to write with a watch (I have so much time on my hands); and there's some kind of leisure there, too, like at the end of a long day when he walks through a plaza under the swaying palms wearing a nice short-sleeve shirt, his brown wrist shiny with a watch.

Chronology: Most mornings I create my special logos of time. I love to lose minutes, hours, a whole morning slipping past noon, and if truth is told, time itself I hate: I am a watcher of memory. I never wear a watch when I write. I unbuckle the band, fold the leather in my hand like a bird's wings pressed into my palms, let them pulse there for a minute, turn the face down against my wood table, and then, for a moment, watch those wings spread back out, lift and rotate and turn a thousand pulses per second, a hummingbird radiating into my work, my hands, my memories.

Blood Work

He was my father's uncle (perhaps a distant relative or friend but always in memory his uncle). On Sundays, when we lived in Connecticut, my father would drive down an oak-lined avenue to a set of tan-and-aqua green high-rise buildings. There must have been an elevator up to his floor, though when I go back in time I only have a vision of looking up toward the high-rise or being there in his small room. I would probably never have seen the bedroom, the bathroom, and I don't remember a kitchen. There was one room with dark green carpeting, a sitting chair, a round table pushed into the corner, and two chairs. He didn't really need any of the chairs, I suppose, because he was in a wheelchair, always a few feet back from a window without curtains, the shades pulled high, as he looked out toward Hartford.

I don't have a name for this man, and rather than cause my father any worry or pain by asking, the only name I can settle on is *Diabetes*.

He always wore a fedora, a white or yellow guayabera, or simply an undershirt, his hands gripping the wheelchair's arms or folded on his lap. He wore shorts, his thighs smooth and very brown, and sometimes bright white tube socks over his amputated legs, the yellow or blue stripes around the tops of the socks encircling the edges of his thighs. My father and Diabetes talked. He shifted his weight when he wanted to emphasize a memory, stress a phrase, a stub rising from the seat of the wheelchair like a pointing finger. When he wasn't wearing socks, the skin at the end of his leftover legs seemed soft, and his thighs flexed with muscles in the gleaming light falling through the window. There were roundish sores near or above where his knees should have been, the injured skin kidney or island shaped, some of the sores a deep maroon color or tinted lime green.

I wish I could remember anything of their conversations—all the stories, work, memory, drink, women. The weather outside the window. Anything. That small room, in what may have been an assisted-living building, is now silent as I look back on his stubby legs. *Diabetes.* It's all I can hear. Then I hear my father describing how his uncle's legs were slowly taken away, one surgery after another, diabetes and gangrene ravishing his body. Many have diabetes in my father's family, sugar as deep in our blood as the sugarcane planted on the island, as working in those fields, and as sweet as the solace of rum, alcoholism. In my father's eyes there was a moment of imagination as he spoke of what happened to his uncle: as if he could foresee the moment when sugar slowly ate away his own legs or arms, even though he never went to the doctor and didn't even know, at the time, he was diabetic.

My father's uncle died long ago, the amputations rising closer to his hips until there was nothing left to cut away. That was always the story I lived with—once they started cutting away, gangrene set in, and then the amputations continued on until you were just a chunk of meat remembering your butchered body.

*
**

A memory continues to return to me like morning sun breaking through gray clouds after a stormy night: my father in the shower, drops of water splashing on his head and running down his shoulders from the leaking showerhead, his right foot under the faucet gushing hot water as he bends over with a long, thin knife and begins to cut across his big toe. I watch his elbow move in a jerk left to right. I watch the water almost silver slowly falling down his shoulders. I watch how white and cold his skin seems, and even though steam rises around him my father is shaking. I try not to look at his big blue toe, the nail swollen with blood. I hear his grunt become a deep yell.

I am looking in the mirror, looking at a face of wonder I have never seen before, and I wait for something to appear, wait for something to change, wait for a tear to fall, wait for a hair to sprout from my chin, wait for a scream or a laugh to break through my tightly closed lips.

I grip the edge of the sink for a moment, hard, raise my feet off the ground. I turn and walk out of the bathroom.

There is no break in the gray clouds giving way to light explaining why I went into the bathroom to see my father release the blood under his swollen toenail with a butcher knife because in a drunk rage he had kicked over a heavy kitchen table. I was alone with him in the house. Always alone with my father: walking down a cold winter street in the night, standing a few feet back as he stood at a bar, sitting in a living room, working with him in the yard, on a car, or in a field, following him on some quest. Maybe I followed him when he walked through the living room with the knife. Maybe I had to go to the bathroom and found him there. Maybe he called me to bring him a towel, and once I saw him cutting his toenail, I dropped the towel next to the tub and walked out. Maybe, and this seems closer to his working-class drunk personality, he went into the bathroom and started the water so it would get hot, got undressed, stepped into the tub, started to soak his toe under the rushing hot water, and then called for me—*Freddie, Freddie, Freddie*—to bring him his knife from the kitchen (that wooden-handled gray-and-blue-bladed thin knife for slicing meat, cubing pieces of pork or goat or rabbit, cutting off fish heads and scaling them). Freddie, his son, was never too young to work and help his father.

The Puerto Rican House returns, and all the men who gathered there—castaways, marooned on that bluff above the St. Joe River, lost forever in their middle years, with no way to get back to their island home.

I have always imagined that I would die in a very small room, in a cheap apartment or hotel, alone, forgotten, and, if I was lucky, after a hard day's work. I have always kept death close, even though I'm often told I should take much better care of myself so I'll be around for my son. Somewhere—I don't fear this—there's a small room, my own room within my own Puerto Rican House, where one day I still may live. Diabetic. Sitting at a table with a bare bulb overhead. A small window to look out onto the street and catch the gleam and blur of colors as cars pass by. My legs shift, the chair creaks, there is no one else there.

Michigan. An early winter morning. I'm sitting at the kitchen table with my father. I'm drinking coffee, and he has a coffee as well as a bowl of steaming oatmeal and a bottle of insulin and a syringe. He has finally learned he's diabetic, and I am saddened that after all his years of drinking and violent rage, after he's finally arrived to a place where he will stay sober, where he can sit still and quiet and live his life with some sliver of peace, he has to lift his shirt or pull down his pants—every morning—in order to take his shot. I think I'm saddened because I must confront such a change in who my father has become, and there's an even greater silence I can't cross. He lifts his shirt and then lifts the needle toward his stomach. I begin to look away, and he stops. He says, *You don't have to turn away, Freddie*. Nothing more. Just those words. Words I return to, and I turn them over and over and over.

✳

My great-uncle returns. He has such a brown handsome face. Not a mark of worry. Silver-white hair cut short, smooth and glossy with a part over his left eye. He's never old. Alone in my room I look in the mirror, study my face, read the lines. Wonder: how can I make something as elegant and beautiful as my uncle?

✳

I wake up and can't move my ankle, can't put any weight on my right leg. My ankle is pink, puffy, double in size. It's the beginning of my end—gout, visiting an endocrinologist, the diagnosis of diabetes.

I watch what I eat. Walk more. Take different meds until I have the one that doesn't make me so nauseous, doesn't make me vomit in the middle of the night. I stop drinking, create an elaborate fiction of how I'll get better and stop taking medicine. Nights consist of two- or three-hour naps because I have to go the bathroom or wake up in a pool of cold sweat, the back of my shoulders and head drenched.

My doctor walks into the examination room. He looks at the floor, and for such a calm and pleasant man it is shocking to see the anger that disfigures his face. He asks how I feel. *Great,* I say, *I feel great. That's good you feel that way but you are going to die. You will die sooner than you have to because your sugars are much too high.*

When my father cut his toe, I wonder if the pain from kicking over that table warranted the sharper pain he must have inflicted on himself with that knife. Even though he wasn't on insulin at that point in his life, even though he was drinking way too much, he may have had an insight into the danger of his injured toe (and then that led to the rash decision that was more violent, could have led to greater harm). We each carry voices, words, fragments of sentences, images, bits and pieces and even the whole cloth of stories within our blood. No doctor can identify this quantum of blood coursing through our beings. No microscope or MRI can hear this blood. But in each and every one of us it's deeply written within, and over time, if we begin to piece or stitch it together, this blood language becomes a kind of book of the heart that guides us to remember, know, and become someone better than our biological self. This memory of my father rises without will and I cannot ignore it: hours and days pass as I closely listen to it, as I try to read this book of memory, blood, and story. A simple, sometimes sad story of a father, a son, and a knife in a bathroom.

There are times, though, when I don't hear it all; it's simply a part of my unconscious gestures, like caressing the fading scar between my fingers before I pick up a pen and begin to write.

My father may have spent hours and days cutting sugarcane, the bread and soul of his island childhood, and sometimes he did it next to burning fields, the soot of that gray and black smoke smudging his clothes, burning his eyes, sugar in that smoke deep in his being with every breath he took. Sugar was also in his blood, I imagine, because he must've been aware of those in his family with diabetes, and perhaps when he cut his toe that day he thought of his mother's diabetes and he was also remembering those Sundays when he took me to visit his uncle.

*
**

When you have diabetes there are great periods of sadness. You go through so much denial, you continue to ask why, and you avoid watching what you eat and drink, and when you begin to forget to take your meds, it's as if you are willing this misremembering. So you wake up one morning with huge blisters on your legs; or you find round patches of swollen flesh on your shoulder or hand that will move from bright red to a purple bruise over time; or you are constantly fighting flulike symptoms; or you wake up in the early hours before dawn, everything blue and black in the room, your eyes straining with some invisible pressure, and for a moment you accept the fact that you are going blind.

I continue to return to *not turning away*, to wondering about the things we forget, overlook, that second of choosing to avert our eyes. Or maybe I'm returning to acceptance. There are men who have never offered many words to others; they didn't need to talk, maybe they were taught not to talk, not to raise their voices, only to sit silently and invisibly as they gave their bodies, minds, sweat, and souls to work; and, in most cases, expressed themselves only by giving their passions to drink. To migration. Distances. Aloneness. Moving ever so close to being lost forever. The physical toll of their working lives is visible to anyone who looks closely, but I'm becoming more obsessed by the emotional lives they struggled with, that deep current of affect that's so hard to see as it courses through their veins: *blood work*.

There were many strangers whom I encountered and my father said, without doubt, *That's my cousin*. Everyone seemed related to him, and now I feel that I cannot turn away because I must gather all those men who are my relations. All my cousins and uncles, even if it may be, in fact, that we are not related by blood.

Most mornings I prick one of my fingertips and read my glucose. The readings often rise and drop—395, 210, 115, 289—or, better yet, they constantly change, like memory, no matter how hard I try to control my sugars. In one drop I return to a room where my great-uncle sits in a wheelchair telling a story. In another I return to a room where I find an uncle under a bare bulb smiling at me. In another I stand outside a gray house, look up at my uncles staring out onto Third Street as they sit on kitchen chairs and fruit crates, and I wonder about their lives, where they have been and where they'll go. In each drop there's a pulse and a pattern I can't turn away from, words and gestures flowing deep within, and the more I listen to and read this language, the closer I get to understanding the work I still need to do in helping them find their way home. I must ask for their forgiveness. They may have lost their names in a region that did not care for them but their lives were always sown in earth.

I am seven or eight and trying to fix some toy. I catch the edge of a stubborn roll of black electric tape, and when I press the blade of the knife against the tape it slips, jumps, and slices across the webbing between my index and middle fingers, up into my knuckle. I drop the roll of tape. There is no immediate pain, nor do I scream, only give a slight, quiet gasp when I see the bright pool of blood thick and still rising between my fingers. I dash to the bathroom to run water over it and staunch and hide my accident, my stupid mistake, because once my father sees the drops on the floor, the streaks in the sink, and then the wad of toilet paper bunched between my fingers, I will feel a sense of shame deeper and more painful than the cut, since we can't really afford to go to the hospital.

I spread my two fingers across the top of my table. The scar is still visible, written like a hastily scribbled word or a quick, light sketch of a crooked river running between mountain ranges on the edge of a map. I run my other index finger over the scar, and it's as smooth as the rest of my hand, almost gone after some forty years, as if sanded down into my skin's grain, now only the shadow of its former self. I see in memory's window the dark wood and brass pins of the handle, the long blade thin from years of sharpening, and then the speckled splotches of gray and blue and dark maroon splashed along the knife's blade. And I see in that long-ago Michigan bathroom that I may have gently handed my father his knife through the steam rising between us.

Other Side of Memory

The story goes like this: On November 15 my blood pressure was dangerously high for a newborn. Blood rushing hot, a fever, my skin very warm to the touch. They lay me down in an incubator with cold bags of saline wrapped in towels placed around my body and rolled me into an oxygen tent where I spent the next thirty days. Sleeping. Dreaming. Crying. All alone. Alone as the doctor and nurses, my mother and father, waited for my body temperature to drop, for my blood pressure to fall. Remembering: faint scent of spilled saline like the sea drying on my skin on a hot summer day.

There is a photo—black and white—of a pair of hands holding me, my body wrapped in a blanket, the edge of extra fabric pulled around and over my head like a hood, and the pair of white hands. My eyes are closed tight (I look like a monk in prayer). I believe the hands are my mother's, her fingers seem so slender and soft, and she's holding me for the first time, just before they placed me in the incubator and wheeled me into the silver mist of an oxygen tent.

There's another photograph, this one in color, and my father—dressed in a beautiful baby blue shirt—holds me in his brown hands, his hands strong on my head, along my shoulders, perhaps after waiting thirty days, there on a couch one December day, somewhere on the other side of memory, there's this father holding his only son for the first time.

I was scared. You wake up in a place like this, a place you've been trying to avoid for years, and you don't know what happened, or why you are there . . . it's frightening. And alone. That's the main thing. Alone. (Perhaps Larry Brown described in *Dirty Work* what the father and son could've never said, let alone thought, though today the words are almost true.)

Potawatomi Hospital was his temporary home. Later, he would return there because of sicknesses and surgeries, become familiar with its halls, and slowly walk them when he visited family for the last time. Halls full of too many footfalls, smells. He can still see where he had lain: the clear silver oxygen tent, a mist gathering within, clouds bunching up over his boiling body, the incubator and tent wedged into the corner of the room, a wide four-paned window filling with muted winter light. A body already caught in the weather of place, an island unto himself. Voices, tears, languages. Lost in the raging storm of the tent, one might decide he was fated to praise shadows. And the light, a light he wants to grow old in, alone in a room, light falling through the window on his hands, this page, his right hand moving memories into the dark purple letters he sows into the page. And maybe his father, this is the story he needs to remember, reached out, his palm flat against the curtain. Maybe he felt he was touching his son's head, his shoulders, his hands. And he's certain that when his father turned and walked out of the room, his steps were hard and fast because he needed to get a drink or make it on time to work.

PARAÍSO

after Pablo Medina

Every day the birds sing my arrival.
4:30 a.m.: the river murmurs *alba*.
This May's visit Paradise.
A hummingbird whirs the morning's fragrance.
I have made more than dreamed
crowded pages, disappearing ink
(throat ruby, hands blue keys).
The wilted purple gems have lost their bright charms.
I sense the summer's hot light and the river's sharp golden glint.
A broken spade leans against the lichen-speckled pine.
An extra line: *Se acabará*. It will end.
I will not move. I will let it heal in the shadows.

—FRED ARROYO

Acknowledgments

In writing *Sown in Earth: Essays of Memory and Belonging*, I always envisioned the book itself as a form *acknowledgement* for the peoples and places and books and languages that shape my writing. This book, perhaps, is a form of "Acknowledgement" in the key John Coltrane played in recognizing a larger creative and holy spirit. Readers will experience, I hope, how I'm carefully acknowledging antecedents or beginnings for a writing life, and I believe friends and colleagues will note their presence as they read these essays. Franz Kafka once wrote, "Every person carries a room inside himself." Your encouragement helped me return to that room of belonging and write this book of memory.

I thank Devin and Rob for their continued readings, conversations, and friendship.

Pablo, I could not have written parts of this book without your remarkable example, mentorship, and friendship. "Aji Dulce" and "Paraíso" are *abrazos* for you.

Thanks to the St. Lawrence University English Department for the time, space, collegiality, and magical year needed to write this book.

Quite a few years ago, Mark and Richard gifted me a month to write in their cabin, where I drafted the seeds to some of these essays.

Allen, Claudia, and Gaylord are colleagues and friends who have enriched the possibilities of my writing, work, and life as I continued to invent and revise this book in Tennessee.

Thanks to Steve for thoughtfully reading some of these essays.

I am grateful to Jill for sharing experiences, trips, and friendship that have helped me to discover my North Country. And I'm equally grateful to Charles, our son, who wanted to travel on the road, sometimes for more than six weeks, where we'd camp, canoe, fish, and walk, and then sit late in the night by a fire under the stars. Days and nights where I continued remembering and dreaming these essays.

Thanks to Mindy, my copyeditor, for your sympathetic reading of these essays, your imaginative suggestions, and for helping me to revise with greater eloquence and possibility.

Thank you, Amanda and Leigh, for designing such an elegant and beautiful book of words and images.

Much gratitude and thanks goes to my editor, Scott De Herrera. Several years ago you asked what I was working on. I tried to express the memories and essays I was writing. You have been enthusiastic from the very beginning, and I am thankful for your unwavering passion for these peoples, regions, and pages.

The author wishes to thank the editors of the following publications, in which versions of this work appeared: *Bluestem*; *Bulletin: Friends of the Owen D. Young and Launders Libraries*; *The Colors of Nature: Essays on Culture, Identity and the Natural World*; *The Ekphrastic Review*; *Gingerbread House Lit Magazine*; *North Dakota Quarterly*; *Origins Literary Journal*; *Pilgrimage Magazine*; *Rathalla Review*; *Reunion: The Dallas Review*; *Sin Fronteras/Writers without Borders*; *Spry Literary Journal*; *Sweet: A Literary Confection*; *upstreet*; *Watershed Review*; *Wildness*; and *52nd City*.

About the Author

Fred Arroyo is the author of *Western Avenue and Other Fictions* (University of Arizona Press, 2012) and *The Region of Lost Names: A Novel* (University of Arizona Press, 2008). A recipient of an Individual Artist Program Grant from the Indiana Arts Commission, Fred's fiction is a part of the Library of Congress series "Spotlight on U.S. Hispanic Writers." Fred's writing is also included in *Camino del Sol: Fifteen Years of Latina and Latino Writing* and *The Colors of Nature: Essays on Culture, Identity and the Natural World*. In the past decade Fred has driven considerable miles along the northern border of the United States, particularly in Ontario, Quebec, and the Maritimes, where he has camped, walked, canoed, and fished in a real and imagined North Country that's influencing a new collection of short stories and a book of poems. Fred is an assistant professor of English at Middle Tennessee State University.